ANGELS

Life in an Australian Motorcycle Gang in the 60s and 70s.

David King & Maureen Lane

M
MELBOURNE BOOKS

Published by Melbourne Books
Level 9, 100 Collins Street,
Melbourne, VIC 3000
Australia
www.melbournebooks.com.au
info@melbournebooks.com.au

Title: Angels: Life in an Australian Motorcycle Gang in the 60s and 70s.
Authors: David King & Maureen Lane
ISBN: 9781925556834

A catalogue record for this book is available from the National Library of Australia

This book is dedicated
to my mother, Joyce Byron King,
to my mentor, Johnny Wilde, to my brother, Glenn King,
to David Gibbons, to Leanne King and
to all the Angels I have known.

— David King

CONTENTS

ANGELS
M/CC
AUSTRALIA

INTRODUCTION

David King was only ten years old when he met the Angels.

Trying to survive a childhood of poverty and violence, David was intermittently living on the streets of Williamstown when fate brought him to a house in Stevedore Street. There he met a kind-hearted man and a group of older boys and men who shared his love of motorcycles and his need to belong.

The Angels were a local motorcycle club who were mostly associated with the western suburbs of Melbourne in the 60s and 70s. That chance meeting would change David's life.

This is a story full of childhood adventures, street smarts and ingenuity. It is the story of a survivor in a time when violence in the home was commonplace, and of the gang of Angels who took him under their wing, protected him and taught him the value of 'safety in numbers'.

David's story also provides insights into the history of Melbourne's west and the teenage boys and girls who broke free of the norms of the 50s to rebel in the 60s. It is a snapshot of life in a motorcycle gang that had a code of conduct, common interests and specific values, in a time gone by.

Ten-year-old David, like seventeen-year-old David and his friends, got up to a good deal of mischief on those streets of Williamstown and sometimes they fell foul of the law. They often tested the patience of the constabulary but were also treated unfairly and suffered rough treatment at the hands of the law.

The Angels code of 'all for one and one for all' was inclusive of all nationalities in a time of overt racism, and ensured tight bonds grew between this band of rebels and misfits who found a place to belong.

This book acknowledges the Angels who shared David's love of motorcycles and taught him skills and life lessons when home and schools had failed him.

It pays homage to Johnny Wilde, who helped and supported David at a time in his life when he was at his most vulnerable.

David's story offers rare insights into life in a motorcycle gang during that time in history and of a little boy lost, surviving enormous challenges to grow into an exceptionally good man.

Maureen Lane

CHAPTER 1

MOTORBIKES AND MISCHIEF

Poverty is the worst form of violence.
— Mahatma Gandhi

It's been a wild ride with many turns in the road as I look into the rear vision mirror. The freedom of the road. The roar of an engine. The excitement. Sex, Drugs and Rock'n'Roll. It all formed part of my journey but the number one constant in all of it was motorcycles.

My love affair with motorcycles began when I was just a little tacker at Williamstown Beach. In the early 60s, the bikes would be lined up on the side of road, right along the Esplanade with the back wheels next to the curb. I was mesmerised by them as I walked from one to the next checking out the shiny wheels and their incredible, loud noise as they revved. Even in those days I could tell one make from another by the noise they made.

In 1963, I was only about eight years old and loved swimming at Willi beach, but I loved the bikes more.

My old man, Tom King, had a 500cc Ariel Red Hunter that had a wooden box fixed to the side car frame. From the time I was around three years old, I was bundled into that wooden box with my two older sisters whose job it was to make sure I didn't fall out as 'the old man' rode the bike with Mum on the back. He would inevitably stop at a pub somewhere and we would have to wait outside with Mum until he came rolling out of the pub to drive us home. He was always so drunk it's a wonder that wooden box didn't turn into a more permanent one.

My dream to own a bike of my own came true when my best mate, Peter Shultz, and I were mucking about in the swamp near the old Williamstown rubbish tip. The swamp ran along the railway track to the refinery and was a rancid pool full of waterfowl and reeds.

We were about nine years old and loved exploring. We used to go in the water to catch lizards and frogs to frighten my sisters, or to search for something we could turn into a toy. Once we even found a box of stewed apricot and rice baby food in tins that had been discarded in the rubbish. Glenn, Peter and I sat on top of the rubbish pile with our exciting find. I produced my trusty pocketknife and cut the tops off the tins with the others keen to gobble the content down as quickly as I could open them. Glenn and Peter jostled for a position next to me. 'Hey, piss off. I want some too!' was the cry from each of us at different times and I made sure I got my fair share and a bit more. Who knows why those cans had been discarded? We didn't even think about what the consequences might be of eating that stuff. Food was always in short supply at my house and those apricots were manna from heaven to me.

On one of these adventures at the tip, I saw something that looked like a motorbike wheel in the water, so we waded into the swamp and dragged out an old Ariel motorcycle. It only had one thing missing—an engine.

We cleaned that bike up and pushed it for miles and miles around Willi and West Newport. We took turns riding it wearing an old helmet we found—freewheeling down the roads and footpaths, squealing and laughing. We had a great time on that old carcass of a bike. The plan was to get a motor and put it in it to make it run but that never happened. The bike sat in the backyard of my house after we lost interest. The weather took its toll, and what had once been the source of so many hours of entertainment, gradually rotted away.

*

Peter Shultz was my best friend from day one at Newport West Primary School when we were just five years old. We were practically inseparable and the two of us were always coming up with schemes and games to entertain ourselves.

Peter's mum was Mrs Shultz who ran Poon's Chinese Food Café in Footscray. In the 50s and 60s, Poon's and Jimmy Wong's were the only Chinese takeaway food places in the area. People took their saucepans there to get them filled with chow mein, chop suey or some other oriental delight.

Peter and I were good pals who always looked after each other and I spent many afternoons out the back of Poon's with his family after school. Mrs Schultz was kind to me and always made sure I had a meal in my belly. I suspect she knew that my mother had trouble feeding her family on the pittance our old man gave her. I would sit around the table in the kitchen behind the restaurant with my mouth watering as Peter and I watched his old grandma and aunty making the dim sims, wontons and spring rolls. We marvelled as their nimble fingers made their magic until we finally got to sample the goods. Dim sims, wantons, spring rolls—they were all delicious.

Mr Poon worked at the shop. He was Mrs Schultz's cousin and a very old gentleman who spoke in broken English. Sometimes I would grab an extra dim sim off his plate as I went past and then I would run out of the shop to the sound of Mr Poon yelling, 'You fluckin' plick! I catch you! I catch you!'

The next time I saw him he would laugh, wag his finger at me and say, 'You cheeky boy!' It was a game we played. Mr Poon also gave us nicknames: Peter was 'Number One Demon' and I was 'Number Two Demon'.

Peter and I hung out together every day and we were always getting into mischief. We used to go down to Newport Quarry (where the Newport Lakes are now) and watch the drivers of the front-end loader back hoes moving the soil and rocks. When they went home, we climbed into the drivers' seats and worked out how to use a screwdriver to start the engines. We played with those huge machines moving the soil and rocks back to where the drivers had got them from. Those workmen must have wondered what the hell had happened and how all their previous day's work was undone overnight! We laughed and laughed.

We were always scrounging for things to play with or to make. Once we found an old Vanguard car on Willi Back Beach and Peter Shultz produced a hacksaw. Together we removed the roof from that old car, attached a couple of petrol tins for floatation, and carried it into the water. We never gave a thought to any danger. We were playing pirates as we sat in the upturned roof of the car and paddled it out into the bay using planks off an old fence. We were engaged in singing 'Sixteen men on a dead man's chest, ho ho ho and a bottle of rum' when we looked up and saw a container ship bearing down on us. A loud horn sounded.

'What do you think you're doing, you bloody little idiots!' called a voice from the deck.

The container ship brushed by us and we had to contend with the slip stream as we got buffeted around on the waves, hanging on for dear life. By the time the waves settled, we were closer to Port Melbourne than home, so we paddled on to shore.

We were tired and our arms ached after paddling such a long way, so we lay on the sand and caught our breath and laughed as we recounted to each other what had happened.

'Did you see how close that ship came?'

'That bloke was mad! His eyes were popping out!'

'We are the best pirates in the world!'

We congratulated each other on successfully taming the bay.

Soon the weather turned cold and wet, and the bay got really choppy. We ditched the car roof and caught the train back to Willi. Mum never found out about our adventure on the high seas. She would have been upset and worried had she known the kind of things we got up to. Things like braving container ships and sharks.

Another time we found a spot in Kororoit Creek, near the oil refinery, where the water was lovely and warm. Of course, Peter and I stripped off and climbed down the bank of the creek to get into the water. We reclined there in the nude, smoking cigarettes Peter had pinched from his mum, thinking we were royalty, as, it seemed, nobody else knew about this beautiful spot. We often visited our private spa until one day the security guard from the refinery appeared, yelling, 'Get out of that fuckin' water! There's so many chemicals it will make your balls fall off!'

We didn't go back.

We were always doing something to get into mischief. If anyone tried to complain about us, Mum always said, 'Not my boys.' She loved all her kids and always stood up for us.

Mum was a gentle soul who did whatever it took to survive. She met her husband, Tom King, during the war while he was on leave from the British navy. He was English, very charming and he swept her off her feet at the local town hall dance. These were uncertain times and nobody could be sure there would be a tomorrow for most of the lads who went off to war. Tom was to set sail in a few weeks and his future lay in the balance. Mum had known him for only two weeks when she married him.

She knew it was a mistake after the first night, but Mum was stuck in a violent marriage and saw no way of getting out of it. He sailed off towards Japan but, unfortunately, he returned after the war, settled in Australia and they had my two sisters before I arrived.

I never refer to Tom King as my father. I usually call him the old man or the old bastard. He was cruel to Mum and to us kids and we often had nothing to eat in the house. I would regularly sit on the steps of the RSL in Newport and wait for him to come out so I could ask him for money to give to Mum so we could eat. Sometimes he obliged. Sometimes I just got a backhander for embarrassing him in front of his mates. He was cruel and mean and usually punished us with a closed fist—Mum copped that too. I ended up in hospital a few times with broken bones and other injuries. Of course, he could be charming, especially to women, but with us he would just blow up for no apparent reason. It was like walking on eggshells in our house—you never knew if he was going to snap.

Growing up, we had a little brown dog called Big Ears that followed us kids everywhere. Mum always knew which house we were visiting because the dog would be waiting for us outside that house. When the day came that we couldn't find Big Ears, we searched everywhere. We asked Pam's boyfriend, Bowie, if he had seen our dog.

'I went rabbiting with Tom,' Bowie said. 'He took Big Ears with us, shot him, and left his body in a paddock.'

Bowie was visibly upset when he told us. The tears flowed from all of us. We loved that dog—we never knew why the old man did it and were too scared to ask.

'Home' was a violent, scary place for Mum as well as for us kids. Mum loved to read and that was her salvation—she would escape into her books to shut out the reality of her life while we were left to our own devices, and we spent a lot of time on the streets. Mum had been a university graduate in the 40s, so she was very highly educated for those times, and yet, she found herself trapped in that two-bedroom weatherboard house with Tom King and eight kids. There wasn't much room: we slept two to a bed and my sisters slept in the lounge room.

The tiny, ramshackle building that housed all of us was an embarrassment to Mum and we were never allowed to invite other kids over to play. Not only that, but Mum never knew when the old man would come home in a bad mood and take it out on her or on us, so she wouldn't let visitors inside the house. Sometimes we had friends in the shed in the yard, though. That was where some of us kids slept at different times, even though it had no door, so no privacy. It was stinking hot in summer and freezing cold in winter, too.

Glenn, Dale and David in the backyard of the family home.

Inside the weatherboard house it was very cramped, with rubbish everywhere. In the bathroom there was only an enamelled metal bathtub, and it wasn't until much later that a shower cubical was added, but it wasn't connected and served as a depository for junk until I was old enough to go to work and fix it.

Mum loved her kids, but she had enough trouble looking after herself, let alone the house and her family. There was seldom enough to eat, and she would often give us what little she had, going hungry herself.

Our clothes were hand-me-downs from Mrs Meddlecott, who lived in the next street. She was a friend of Mum's who had grandchildren a little older than us. She would bring their old clothes to our house which caused great excitement as we rummaged through the plastic bags to get our 'new' clothes and shoes. We wore them until they fell off our backs.

We really had no supervision when we were growing up. Poor Mum. She did her best, but she was fragile and in an intolerable situation. My older sisters did the best they could, too, but they were just kids.

When I was eight years old, Mum went into hospital to rest before she had the twins and the neighbours came in to help out with a spring clean. During that time, my two younger brothers, Glenn and Dale, and I were put into a boy's home in Queenscliff as there wasn't anyone to take care of us.

As the car drove us up to the gates, we were very apprehensive, and with good cause. We stood on the steps and looked up at the huge building in front of us, when a voice spoke.

'Welcome to Cottages by the Sea,' the woman said with a fake smile.

She seemed to be the boss. I was to have many run-ins with her over the next few weeks. At one stage she called me a 'little gutter snipe' and, although I had no idea what it meant, I knew it wasn't good, so I called her an 'old hag'. Her eyes narrowed and her mouth puckered into what I called a 'cat's bum face', and she walloped me for that.

I hated it there but at least they fed us—even if dinner involved Brussels sprouts. None of us liked them and we used to hide them in our pockets to later dispose in the garden. Needless to say, we got caught and landed ourselves in trouble again.

Bath time was an ordeal. I didn't mind going in the bath with my brothers, but not with strangers. We had to line up like a production line outside the bathroom, waiting our turn to get into the water. I always tried to be up the front of the line because they used the same water for about twenty kids. If I got in first, I could be sure that nobody before me had peed in the water—or worse. The staff had a hell of a time getting Glenn into the bath. He fought them and wouldn't go. It was hard enough to get him in a bath at home, let alone with a tribe of other boys.

My brothers and I didn't cope very well with the regimentation. It was supposed to be emergency relief for families and the kids were supposed to be on holiday from orphanages all around the state.

We were used to pretty much doing as we pleased at home. Here, we were bossed around and had to do chores like make the bed, pick up rubbish and sweep the floors. These tasks were all alien to us. It didn't seem like much of a holiday and we felt cheated that they got us there under false pretences. We were also homesick for Mum.

I met my mate Colin in the home, and we were to stay mates for the next forty years until his death in 2016. We palled up and played together in the old tram that was in the backyard.

When I first met Colin in the home, he told me that there was a 'monster' at his orphanage, a paedophile, who was out to 'get' him. Colin hid in a cupboard one night with a carving knife, ready to defend himself. After that, the monster didn't bother him and moved on to someone else.

On Sundays, the staff marched us up to the Presbyterian Church in town. We were not used to churches but we knew we were supposed to be Catholics, so we didn't want to go to the Presbyterian service. We were told in no uncertain terms that we had no choice and so we toddled off in line with the others to the service.

We all missed our mum and our sisters, although little Dale didn't seem to mind being there as much as Glenn and I did. We started to look for opportunities and ways to escape, but they were few and far between. Glenn was caught up doing chores when my chance came, so I took off without him and climbed over the rough wooden fence.

I'd had enough of 'prison' life and started to walk home on my own. As I wandered along the water where the highway followed the coast, a man saw me and stopped his car.

'Hey, kid! Where are you going?' he asked.

'I need to catch a train,' I said, 'I'm going home.'

The elderly man was on his way to Geelong, so he gave me a lift to the station where I caught the train to Melbourne.

All through the early part of the train journey I kept my head down or looked out the window, avoiding eye contact with anyone. Then I saw that a ticket inspector was making his way down the aisle, so I thought quickly and went to sit with a family of kids who were travelling with their mother, and I talked to them. I nervously waited for someone to say, 'Who are you with, little boy?' but nobody took any notice of me and the ticket collector walked on by. I made it to Melbourne, then caught another train home without being detected.

The police were waiting for me there.

'You little bastard!' the constable said and, although I screamed and yelled, he grabbed me by the scruff of the neck, flung me in the back of the police car and off to the police station we went.

I don't remember being scared at the cop shop. I was just angry that I didn't get to stay home with Mum, even if only for a little while. Later, a young copper drove me back to Queenscliff without a word.

When I got back to the home, Glenn was angry with me and we had a bit of a scuffle in the dirt until he calmed down and I could tell him about my adventure. He could never stay mad at me for long.

We stayed at Queenscliff until a neighbour came to take us back home to meet one of the twins and to be with Mum after the funeral of the other twin. Mum was as sad as I had ever seen her. I don't think she ever got over the death of baby Paul, who was twin to Peter, our new baby brother.

Before the boys' home, school hadn't worked out as I had wanted it to. As a five-year-old, I had longed to go to Sacred Heart Catholic Primary in Newport because my friend Brian was going there. The children on the other side of those gates always looked happy and I longed to be part of the games they played in the yard. Brian took me with him to the orientation day and I loved it. We sang songs and did activities and the teachers gave each of us a coloured block which we were able to take to the canteen to exchange for a mug of tomato soup and a bread roll. I thought that was fantastic. They were just nice people and I loved everything about it. It was as good as I had thought it would be and I wanted to belong there with all my being.

I was all talk about it when I got home, and I was so excited. But the old man said, 'You are not going there. We don't have the money!' My dreams were shattered, and I cried and cried. I didn't understand how Brian, who had the same number of siblings in his family as us, and was 'in the same boat' financially, could go but I couldn't.

I later found out that my old man had gone to a Catholic school in England and had been expelled for setting a nun on fire. I was surprised he went to a Catholic school, but not about the last bit.

I ended up going to Newport West Primary and that was where I first met Peter Schultz. Peter came to school on that very first day dressed in Lederhosen, which inspired the other kids to make fun of him; not only because of his funny leather shorts, but because he was half-Chinese and wearing funny leather shorts. I hooked up with him because other kids were picking on him. I was short for my age and feeling very out of place, so we teamed up and formed a mateship that lasted thirty-one years.

Newport Primary School was tough. I couldn't read as well as the other kids and got bullied by students and teachers alike. The teachers victimised my brothers and sisters too, because of our shabby clothes and the plastic sandals we wore in summer and winter—rain or shine.

I soon just gave up and stopped trying to learn. My embarrassment at school turned into defiance. A kid will always rather be thought of as bad than dumb, so I started to act up and cause trouble at school. Teachers reacted in the same way the old man did—with violence. It didn't matter to me. They could strap me and I would laugh at them and they would get mad and hit me again, but I got worse than that at home, so it was like water off a duck's back.

Class photo: David is back row on the left.

The situation at home worsened and became intolerable. I gathered a gang of mostly ten and eleven-year-olds, plus my brother Glenn (who was nine). Peter Shultz, the Smith brothers (Billy, Peter and another Glenn), and others hung around with me and made up the gang.

Williamstown was a working class, seaside village next to where I lived in Newport and it was the next stop along the train line. It was and still is a very historic and beautiful place. It was the site of the first European settlement and is still full of bluestone buildings with convict markings on the stones. I had jumped on the train many times to get there and sometimes I walked, so I knew every street and laneway very well.

I started running wild in those streets and back lanes of Williamstown. It was safer than home for Glenn and me, and we had my pals for company during the day. Sometimes I slept under the bandstand in Commonwealth Gardens Reserve at night while Glenn most often went home. Musical instruments were kept in the room under the bandstand, but we didn't take them. We played them a bit, just messing around with the tubas, drums and trombones.

Sometimes we went into the old morgue—we picked the lock on the chain and slept in there on the slabs. It was a small bluestone building where the dead bodies had been kept in the early days of European settlement. Inside it was dark and cold, but at least I was safe and dry, and nobody was going to disturb me in the night. We weren't scared of ghosts or anything, we just needed somewhere to sleep in bad weather.

In the warm weather we slept out in the open in Willi Gardens or Commonwealth Reserve, looking up at the stars and talking about the footy. Teddy Whitten was a champion player for my team, the Footscray Bulldogs. He was a local hero and he lived close by. One night, as we lay in the park under the stars, Glenn said, screwing up his nose, 'Did you see Teddy Whitten walking his dog? He's got a bloody poodle! He should have a bulldog.'

'Yeah,' I said. 'I saw him the other day and yelled out to him,

"Hey, Ted! Where's your bulldog, you bloody pansy!'"

We laughed at the thought of big tough Teddy Whitten walking a coiffured little poodle.

'Did he say anything back?' asked one of the other kids.

'He called me a little bastard and said he would catch me and give me a kick up the arse!'

We all had a laugh and then settled down to sleep.

It was quite good sleeping out in the warm weather on the grass with my mates. A bit like camping. There was only one time I ever got hurt in a park and that involved a cockatoo and an owl.

We had a pet cockatoo at home. His name was George and he had the run of the house, except on the occasions when we went out in the car. Glenn and I didn't like to put him in the cage, we thought it was like being in prison for him. So, one Sunday, when we went visiting relatives, Glenn and I put his chain on his leg and we attached that chain to a big wooden kitchen chair. The intention was to stop George from following us and we thought he would be fine chained to the chair with his water dish, but George had different ideas. When we came home, we discovered that George had been a very busy bird. He got loose and chewed right through the back of the chair and had eaten a hole through the backdoor of the house. When we got home, we found a very happy cockie gorging on parrot food in the laundry.

Eventually, George died and so, one night, when Peter Schultz and I were in Paine Reserve in Newport just mucking around, we saw a beautiful barn owl in one of the trees. A plot hatched in my mind. I thought it would be a good idea to have a pet owl. After all, I already had George's cage for the owl to live in. I decided to climb the tree and catch him.

I could see his heart-shaped, white face with his beady eyes watching me as I managed to shimmy up the tree and stop behind him. He stayed still. I reached out my hand and grabbed him.

I didn't know owls could turn their heads right around, nor did I know that their beaks were so sharp. That owl bit right through my fingernail and nearly took the top of my finger off. I was up the tree swearing and cursing that bloody owl when it finally let go of my finger and flew away, unperturbed.

Peter was rolling on the ground with his feet kicking in the air, holding his stomach and laughing his head off while I fell out of the tree hanging onto my bleeding finger. 'Shut up! Shut up! The bloody bird ate my finger!' I screamed at him. George's cage would have to remain empty, and my finger never fully recovered.

*

Peter Schultz, my brother Glenn and I were always looking for adventures and not all of them were as dangerous as the one with the owl.

We, like most kids of that era, watched *The Swamp Fox* on TV and loved to take turns at pretending we were the Swamp Fox—an activity which inspired lots of mischief around the streets of Williamstown. *The Swamp Fox* was a Disney TV show based on a real-life American Revolutionary War hero, Francis Marion, who evaded the Redcoats by hiding in the swamps. We sang:

Swamp Fox, Swamp Fox, tail on his hat
Nobody knows where the Swamp Fox at

Swamp Fox, Swamp Fox, hiding in the glen
He'll ride away to fight again
Got no money, got no beds, got no roof above our heads
Got no shelter when it rains. All we've got is Yankee brains

We wagged school a lot and played that Swamp Fox game, pinching fruit from the fruit stall or from local gardens and scrounging for things we could sell to get money to buy food, then quickly running off. Peter always had plenty to eat but not Glenn and me—we were always hungry.

One day, when we were scrounging around Williamstown, we found an unattended keg of beer behind the Customs House Hotel and rolled it away.

We had no idea how to open it and knocked the ball down into the keg using a cricket bat handle. It exploded like a volcano and we were squealing and running around with our faces upturned and our mouths open getting soaked in beer. We must have looked pretty funny—little urchins running about excitedly and being drenched in beer and laughing. I'm sure the publican from Custom's House Hotel wouldn't have seen the joke, though.

The local coppers used to know we were up to no good and chased us through the streets many times. We were fast and knew all the little alleys, scampering down the lanes to get away. 'I'll get you King boys!' was ringing in our ears as we laughed, 'No you won't!' In our minds we were the Swamp Fox evading the Redcoats.

We would be gone for days. When we knew the old man was at work, we went home so we could see Mum and the other kids a couple of times a week. As I said, there was often no food in the house, so we used to pinch the milk from the doorsteps of the neighbours' houses. The milkman found out what we were doing and, after that, he used to give us milk to drink so we wouldn't steal the milk from other people. Sometimes he even gave us chocolate or strawberry flavoured milk. He must have been a kind soul. His name was Mr Tribe and he had a draught horse that pulled the milk cart. He had a couple of kids himself and I hung around with them sometimes. When Mr Tribe was out, we used to take the horses out in his backyard and ride them. That was great fun.

The iceman used to make deliveries in our street too. He would chip off a piece of ice and throw it to us kids. One hot day, the iceman gave us a big block of ice. We took it in a hessian bag to the Newport railway station underpass. We put the bag on top of the ice block to sit on and slid down the dip in the path squealing with laughter. We did that until the ice block melted and our bums were sore. It's a wonder we didn't get frostbite on our balls.

Once Glenn climbed up into an ice machine to get some ice out. When he tried to shimmy back down the chute with the ice block, panic gripped his face.

'I'm stuck!' he said.

We tried everything to get him out. We grabbed him by the feet and pulled. Nope. He wouldn't budge.

'We're gonna get in the shit for this!' I said.

We exhausted all other options before the fire brigade had to come to get him out. They arrived with the police and we were all marched home. Thankfully, the man who owned the ice factory wasn't upset. He stifled a smile as he said, 'I don't want to press charges, officer.'

The policeman marched us home, but Mum just said, 'Naughty boys. Don't do it again. I don't want you getting hurt.'

top left: Sisters Pam and Terry with David and Glenn.

top right: David's mother—Joyce King.

bottom left: David on the mudguard of the family's first car with sister, Pam.

bottom right: David (kneeling) with brothers Glenn and Dale. Glenn was sulking because he wanted to hold the gun when they were going rabbiting.

CHAPTER 2

TINKERING AND TECH SCHOOL

I have trouble with names and faces, but I never forget a car.
— *The Love Bug*, 1968

My sisters, Pam and Terry, took care of me sometimes and, after they got married and moved out of the house, I spent a lot of time with them at their homes. In Terry's backyard was an old Chevy (1948 light truck) that belonged to a friend of hers, so Peter Shultz and I decided we would fix it up and get it going.

Nobody would have believed that two roustabout twelve-year-old kids could make that happen, but we actually did it. We got that engine to roar. It was such a buzz that I knew it was what I wanted to do for the rest of my life—mess around with engines and make them roar.

We took the Chevy for a ride up the street and into the paddocks where we bumped and thumped over rocks and tufts of long grass, laughing and doing donuts in the dirt, but when we got back to Terry's place there was an angry line-up waiting for us. Terry, her husband, and the guy who owned the car were there with the two big policemen—all with frowns on their faces.

We had defied the odds to make that car run, but the owner was pissed off that we took it for a joy ride. We got a tongue lashing but no charges were laid, and we still felt pretty pleased with ourselves.

With confidence bolstered, we got an old FC Holden from a lady in West Newport. It had been her husband's car and no-one in her family wanted it. It had been rotting away and she was glad to get rid of it, so she sold it to us boys—me, Glenn and a friend, Chris.

We got it going and we used to drive it to school and park around the corner from the entrance. We picked up other kids on the way and we even had kids riding in the boot sometimes. We were about thirteen years old at this time and eventually we got caught when someone dobbed us in, so we couldn't drive on the roads anymore. That didn't stop us taking it to the paddocks and driving until it blew up.

After our primary school experiences, I went to Williamstown Technical School where I learnt fitting and turning, sheet metal work and woodwork, but no mechanics, which disappointed me greatly. Peter Schultz's parents sent him to Williamstown High School in an attempt to break us up. That was never going to work—we continued to meet up after school.

Throughout my school life, no-one seemed to care about me, except the principal at Williamstown Tech, Mr Morrison. I spent a lot of time outside his office, but he was kind to me; he just let me sit there and never hit me. I suspect he knew what was going on at home and had some sympathy for our situation.

One of the teachers at school was the famous athlete, Peter Norman, an Olympic runner who held the title of the 'fastest white man alive'. In the 1968 Olympic Games, he stood on the podium in solidarity with Tommie Smith and John Carlos when they made their powerful protest against racism with raised fists in a 'Black Power' salute at the medal ceremony.

Mr Norman taught Physical Education at my school. One day I was being a bit disruptive and swore at him, then ran away. He took off after me, but he couldn't catch me. He told the principal, 'That kid is like a little jack rabbit darting and changing direction.' I held my head down and tried not to smile, but I couldn't help it.

Williamstown Technical School.

In 1968, I was thirteen and in art class when the teacher said, 'King! Use that metal dustpan and brush to clean the floor.' I was bending down doing just that, but I must have been singing or something when the teacher walked up behind me and punched me in the back of the head. I spun around with the dustpan still in my hand and hit him on the side of the head near his temple. It was a reflex action, but he went down like a sack of spuds and was out cold. There was a hushed silence as

I looked down at him with my eyes wide. The shock of what I had done left me in a panic. The silence turned into a collective gasp, followed by bedlam as all the kids stood on the seats to get a better look. Laughing, they started high-fiving each other.

The police were called, and the school wanted to lay charges, but when the police took statements from the other kids and heard what had happened, they told my mum that she should lay charges against the teacher. Of course, she wouldn't do that.

The principal was sympathetic, but he said, 'I understand you were only retaliating, but I have a responsibility to support my staff. I'm really sorry, David.'

And after those words, I was expelled.

After that, my self-education continued as I spent my time messing around with engines that I found, and I learnt the rudiments of mechanics by watching other people work.

One day, an old man in Yarraville gave Peter and me a Mark11 Zephyr ute that was blocking his driveway. He wanted it gone so he asked us to take it and we were very keen, but there was a big problem: it had no accelerator. Peter and I worked out that if we attached a string to the carburettor and I operated that, Peter could steer and operate the brake and clutch. We managed to drive that old bomb all the way home to Williamstown, with the string attached, and we fixed it up and had a good car for driving around in the paddocks for a while.

Another of our project cars was a black Vanguard from the 40s that a neighbour gave us to work on. It became such a good car that my old man wanted to take it for himself, so we moved it to Peter's house so the old man wouldn't pinch it.

My brother Glenn and I were both mad keen on motorbikes and we begged, borrowed and stole money to save up to buy a BSA 250 motorcycle from another kid we knew. It had a clapped-out magneto, so we took the magneto to a man in Newport who had lots of bikes that he worked on. He produced another clapped-out magneto and we married up the parts to make a good one and got the bike going. We rode that bike for ages.

One day, we rode around a corner as a bus was going past. We didn't stop in time and went BANG! Right into the side of the bus. We jumped up and ran away, pushing the bike while the bus driver chased us, swearing and waving his arms at us. The passengers on the bus yelled at him to 'leave the kids alone' and he gave up the chase after only a few metres.

We were riding that bike later when a policeman pulled us over. He told us, 'You can't fool me by wearing helmets.' He knew we were only kids because of our slight frames. He let us off with a warning but, of course, that didn't stop us. We kept riding it. Eventually, the engine blew up and the man who gave us the magneto bought the bike from us.

There was a dirt-bike track on the abandoned Williamstown Racecourse. Kids used to ride motorbikes there because it was quite isolated and flat with a go-cart track near the creek. The police didn't mind if we rode the motorbikes or we drove paddock bombs so long as we pushed the bombs or bikes along the roads to get there. We would find old cars in people's yards and offer to get rid of them. Sometimes money changed hands, or we made a swap for something else, then we went to work fixing the mechanisms and pushed our vehicles, puffing and blowing, along the roads to drive them. We had great fun on the tracks—we either rolled the car over or the engine blew up. Lots of us did this kind of thing to occupy ourselves; there wasn't much else to do. We used to see snakes there and my mate Colin ran over one once on a motorbike. It flicked up and landed on his seat, its tail wrapped around the mudguard and its upper half on the seat behind him. Just as he turned his head and saw it, it tried to bite him on the arse. He just dropped the bike on the ground in a panic and got a stick to dispatch the snake with some sharp blows to the head.

I developed pretty good mechanical skills for a kid. As I said, I used to watch others fix engines and I learnt from them. From the age of about ten, my skills had been nurtured by a most unexpected source.

CHAPTER 3

A NEW FAMILY

Four wheels move the body. Two wheels move the soul.
— Laconia Harley Davidson

In the summer of 1965, I went exploring down a back lane and discovered a row of motorbikes in Stevedore Street, Williamstown. I went to investigate. Inside a huge shed that had once been an industrial laundry factory floor, I met a man who changed my life. His name was Johnny Wilde. Johnny was a short, thin man with dark, wavy hair styled like Elvis Presley. I discovered that Johnny ran a business out of that old laundry. He fixed up old motorcycles and sold them. That day in Stevedore Street, this scruffy little urchin became his new fixer upper project. He took me under his wing and taught me a lot about motorcycles and about life in general but, most of all, he taught me what it was like to be part of a family.

In 2020, when I asked Johnny about our first meeting, this is what he said:

> The first time I saw David I thought, 'Who's this little larrikin?' He wasn't a bit scared to walk into the workshop. After that first day, David and his brother Glenn used to come down to the factory floor and hang around there and be a bit of a nuisance. I used to give them jobs to do like rubbing down chassis or cutting up handlebars. We had a jig to make those. I always gave them something to do. Glenn went home but David was at our place all the time sleeping on the couch. He was a little larrikin.
>
> I watched Johnny strip motorcycles and put them back together. I helped him where I could. I didn't go home much and stayed at his place with him and his wife, Marion, and their little baby, Johnny Junior. 'What's going on with this kid?' Marion would say. 'Doesn't anyone miss him?' I'm sure Mum missed me, but she had seven other kids to worry about and the old man wouldn't care if I was there or not.

Johnny let me hang around his house and his workshop, and Marion fed me. It was such a treat to have food on the table and watch how this little family interacted. Best of all, I had found a safe place at last.

I loved being there with the bikes and watching the comings and goings of the bikies who turned up to help out or hang out. The atmosphere was so relaxed and certainly not what I was used to at home. I came to think of Johnny like a big brother and Marion always showed me kindness and looked after me. I was just a kid, but I was a bit in love with her. One day I was messing around on a motorbike and one of the guys said to me, 'Get off that bike! You can't ride it. You're too little.' I decided to prove him wrong. I started the engine and climbed onto the seat. I rode it alright but couldn't stop and rode right through the bathroom door at the back of the house.

Marion was just getting out of the tub and clutching a towel. She started screaming, 'Get out! Get out!' My mouth was open and my eyes were like saucers. I was even more in love with her after that.

Johnny Wilde.

Johnny also worked as a plumber for Carlton & United Brewery and he visited hotels to fix any problems with beer taps and pipes. He used to take me along with him to work. I sat in the pubs and drank lemon squash while he fixed the plumbing. I loved going with him.

The big love in Johnny's life was motorcycles and he got along with everyone, so he was very easy to be around. He would talk to me and tell me stories about his life: 'I got my licence when I was about eighteen, I think. I went riding with two motorcycle coppers and they took me into the city for my test. The two cops ran a yellow light and I thought, "They are trying to trip me up here." So I did the hand signal for stop and waited for the lights to change. When I caught up to the coppers they said, "What did you stop for? We know you can ride. Just keep up. We've got shopping to do!"'

He told me this story once or twice. I never got sick of listening to him.

Friday nights, Johnny and I would go to *The Age* newspaper office in Melbourne to get in first to buy a copy of the following day's paper with the bikes for sale. On Saturdays, we would be on someone's doorstep to buy a bike. Another member of the Angels, Chicken Man, would come with us. He got his nickname because he would often drink too much and pass out in the old chicken coop at the back of Johnny's place. Chicken Man remembered going to *The Age*'s office with us:

> Dave and me were pretty thick from the start. We used to go to *The Age* in the early hours of the morning to get the bargains in the paper. There was a rubbish bin outside *The Age* office that used to catch fire in winter—spontaneously combust—and we would stand around it to get warm while we waited for the bargains in the newspaper. The coppers complained a couple of times, about the spontaneous combustion, but they got used to it and left us alone.

After securing a bargain, we would take the bikes back to Johnny's place to work on them.

My old man did turn up, once, to drag me home and give me a beating. I think Mum must have been worried and sent him to look for me because he wouldn't have done that off his own bat. He never cared about what happened to me.

That day, there were four or five Angels hanging out in the workshop, along with Redder from another gang—the Derelicts.

The old bastard marched in and started threatening me: 'What do you think you are doing, you little bastard! Get over here!' and he tried to grab hold of me to give me a beating. The Angels and Redder all stood up and formed a line between him and me.

'He's quite safe being here at my house. We watch over him,' said Johnny. The old bastard was motionless with fists clenched for a minute as he sized up the situation. The Angels looked at him—they were not going to take a backward step.

The old bastard turned on his heel and left with steam coming out of his ears. I felt relieved and safe. The Angels had protected me. I was also surprised to see the old man intimidated and back down. That day he got a bit of his own medicine. I smiled—inside and out.

He left me alone after that and I visited Mum at home when he wasn't there.

*

Around this time, Johnny, Marion and their three babies moved to Roberts Street, Spotswood. There was a house in front of an old dairy which soon became Johnny's new workshop—Westgate Choppers.

The Angels and lots of other guys started hanging out in that old dairy and in the stables that had an entrance from the back lane as well as the front of the dairy. That meant the boys could bring their bikes directly into the workshop to work on them and avoid going through the front of the house.

Tappets was a member of the Critters Motorcycle Club. He recalled hanging out at both of Johnny's places:

> My first encounter with Johnny was in Stevedore Street, Williamstown in 1969, as a twelve-year-old, fresh out of institutions and on crutches after a spinal operation and six months in a plaster cast.
>
> I lived 'round the corner in Douglas Parade and the sound of the bikes caught my attention. I followed the sound to Johnny's place down a back alley where

> John, David and the other Angels befriended me. Many a great memory as a teenage kid at the bikie parties and in Wildey's workshop where l would help him sand down bike tanks and help bend ape-hangers as he started Westgate Choppers.

Everyone worked on their bikes and helped each other out. The dairy had a warm, friendly atmosphere and I loved the banter between friends:

'What are you doing with that heap of shit!'

'Get yourself a decent bike, ya fuckwit!'

They were always trying to outdo each other with insults about how they looked or how they smelled!

'What are you doing, you ugly prick!'

'Haven't you got any bloody soap at home! Get away from me or have a wash!'

Once when Chicken Man was passed out, I glued his shoes together with epoxy resin. When he woke up the next morning and tried putting them on his feet, he had no hope!

'What arsehole did this?' he said, looking around the room. He knew straight away who did it because I was pissing myself laughing. He chased me around the dairy, laughing, and shaking his fists. 'I'll kick your arse, you little turd,' he threatened, but he didn't catch me. He was to get even with me later though when I sat on a seat in my new jeans and found it had been newly painted.

Westgate Choppers was a great place to be and, finally, Chicken Man had a bedroom. It might have been in the stables where the horses had been kept but it was one step up from the chicken coop, I reckon. Later, Johnny would move into a proper factory off Kororoit Creek Road, North Williamstown, but for now, the dairy was home.

Johnny had a remarkable talent for airbrushing motorcycles and was in great demand. Local identity, Barry Hanson lived in Altona—a neighbouring suburb of Newport. He remembered going to see Johnny Wilde work on his mate's motorcycle tank:

> My mate Laurie lived down the lane from Westgate Choppers. When I visited him, he took me to meet Johnny Wilde and he was working on airbrushing a motorbike. It was a snake wrapped around the fuel tank and it was just so awesome. I'd never seen anything like it before or since. He was so talented.

I learnt a lot from Johnny about life, about motors and spray painting, and about being part of a different kind of family. Johnny was the dad I wished I had, although he wasn't old enough to be my father.

CHAPTER 4

MOTORCYCLE CLUBS

A BRIEF HISTORY—BEFORE MY TIME

Animals travel on all fours. Mankind on two. Motorcycling is not a means of transport but an ideology, a nomadic way of life.
— Amit Reddy

From 1954, the Angels were just a bunch of guys who loved motorcycles and got together at Williamstown Beach where I had seen their bikes when I was a little tacker walking along The Esplanade.

A few of the guys came from Footscray, Sunshine and other places further afield to hang out in Williamstown, and eventually they formed Angels Motorcycle Club. Johnny Wilde was an original member and leader of the club. Although the Angels shared a name with the more infamous gang that originated in the US (Hells Angels), the local Angels had no connection with that group.

Any bloke of any ethnicity who wanted to join the Angels was welcomed. It was all about having fun—just hanging out together and riding or drinking. I was never afraid of the blokes. Not even the ones who looked a bit scary with tattoos, long beards and moustaches. I loved hanging out with them and they made a fuss of me. I felt safe.

Original Angel's patch owned by a Life Member—nicknamed 'Knackers'.

Johnny said: 'In those early days, it was pretty tame. They were more likely to get wasted on a bottle of Green's Ginger Wine than on drugs or anything else.'

During the 50s, after World War II, there was a strong economy and full employment which meant more families could afford cars and motorcycles. Some returning dispatch riders and others who had experienced riding motorbikes in the military continued to ride when they came back home. Motorcycles really do get into your blood.

A high level of skill is needed to ride a motorcycle. You need to juggle the noise and the speed while assessing the danger around every curve. It is a combination of balance, strength, and knowledge of mechanics that makes a skilled rider, and riding is very addictive. Following the road, with the wind blowing across your face, and feeling free and wild while in control of a big heavy machine is a buzz. Being instantly recognised as a motorcyclist commands a kind of respect too.

Angels gather in a local park.

Back in 1953, Marlon Brando starred in the movie *The Wild One.* His character inspired a generation of motorcycle riders to don a uniform of jeans, t-shirts, boots and the signature leather jacket. Guys gathered together to live the dream. With their greasy, slicked-back hair, they looked the part cruising the streets. Individuals met up, became friends, and then formed groups to ride together. Eventually those groups became clubs all over Australia.

In 1954, a race track was opened on the site that is now Cherry Lake in Altona and people raced cars and motorcycles there. The Harley Davidson Motorcycle Club of Australia held the first race meeting on that site for motorcycle enthusiasts and the Marlon Brando wannabes flocked there in droves. Car races were held at the lake circuit, too, and boasted champions Jack Brabham and Jack Jones as participants in car racing events.

The Harley Club formed on 5 February 1924, at the Ritz Café, Lonsdale Street, Melbourne, when their first meeting was held. It was commonplace to name clubs after certain motorcycle makes in those days and Melbourne already had clubs with names such as A.J.S, Norton, Indian, and Rudge, so Harley joined the ranks.

Angels at Bathurst motorcycle races in New South Wales.

Car racing events were held at the Fishermen's Bend Airstrip, 'Riverside', from 1949 and continued through until 1960, when a deteriorating track surface was no longer suitable for the increased speed of competing cars and motorcycles. Drag racing events took over the track and were organised by the Victorian Hot Rod Association. Drag races were held from 1962 through to 1966 until the track was no longer safe.

Calder Park Raceway was founded in the farming community of Diggers Rest circa 1966. What began as a dirt track carved into a paddock by a group of like-minded, motoring enthusiasts wanting to create a place to race their FJ Holdens, underwent many changes over the years to cater for different forms of car and motorbike racing.

Motorcycle racers at Cherry Lake, mid-50s.

NEW £35,000 SPEED TRACK TO OPEN

RECORD CROWDS EXPECTED AT ALTONA ON SUNDAY

The fastest speeds yet clocked in Australia should be recorded at the new £35,000 Altona motor racing circuit when it opens on February 21. The opening meeting will be conducted by the Harley Club of Victoria. Australia's leading motor cycle stars will compete at the meeting.

A special feature of the meeting will be a time trial race between Stan Jones, crack Australian racing car driver, and Frank Sinclair, national motor sidecar driver.

Jones will race in his Cooper Special and Sinclair on a Vincent Special. Both vehicles are capable of more than 130 mph.

It will be the first time in the world that a racing car and racing bike have competed in a time trial.

The new track, which cost £35,000, was built by well-known racing drivers Stewart and Neil Charge and is the first of its kind to be built in Australia.

They have laid more than 2¼ miles of all weather bitumen track fully enclosed by a steel safety fence. Modern sanitary conveniences have been installed and future plans provide for stands, changing rooms, fully equipped racing pits and permanent refreshment rooms.

Free parking space is available for 3000 cars.

By rail the track is only a few hundred yards from Altona and Seaholme stations. By tona and Seaholme stations. By road it is off Geelong Road near Millers Road.

Special buses direct to the track will meet every train at North Williamstown station.

★

Six cases of infections diseases were reported in January—two of scarlet fever and four of pulmonary T.B.

left: Williamstown Chronicle, *19 February 1953.*

right: Champion driver Jack Brabham racing at Cherry Lake, Altona, mid-50s.

Brooklyn Speedway and Melbourne Speedway provided some excitement after the Cherry Lake track closed but the bikes on the tracks were more likely to be race bikes rather than Harleys.

Many different motorcycle clubs sprang up in Victoria. Here is a list of just some of those clubs:[1]

- Angels (not Hells Angels)
- Axemen
- Banshees (now Black Uhlans)
- Black Hearts
- Black Knights
- Black Watch
- Black Widows
- Bohemians (Ballarat, 70s)
- Broke Brothers (now Bandidos)
- Cobras (Bendigo)
- Colonials (Melbourne, 80s/90s)
- Confederates
- Cougars (Horsham)
- Critters
- Deaths Creed
- Degenerates (Melbourne North)
- Deviates
- Devils Outlaws
- Devils Horsemen
- Dominators (Brunswick)
- Dominoes
- Donald Ducks
- Doom Riders
- Fast Company
- Freak Brothers (late 70s)
- Freedoms Shadows (Mount Dandenong area)
- Gorgons
- Heretics
- Loners (Ballarat, now Bandidos)
- Leneva Cribbenfoots (Wodonga)
- Mad Dogs (Shepparton, patched over to Outlaws)
- Nordic Knights (Melbourne, then Beaufort)
- Pagan Saints (Yarraville/Footscray, late 70s to mid-80s)
- Phantoms (Ballarat, 50s)
- Pharaohs (Altona, 70s)
- Rat Pak
- Rats Rectum
- Red Barons (Footscray—Maidston)
- Renegades (Templestowe)
- Resurrected (Morwell, 1976)
- Road Pirates
- Road Rebels
- Saints
- Saints & Sinners

1 List taken from Australian & New Zealand Motorcycle Clubs Register with some local gangs added.

Saracens (Geelong)

Satan's Cavalry (Gippsland)

Satan's Sinners (Moorabbin, now Coffin Cheaters)

The Others MC (Melbourne, mid-80s)

Tribesmen

Tyrants

Undertakers

United Hawks

Vikings (Laverton)

Vigilantes (Glenroy/Pascoe Vale, 1958–64. Not to be confused with the 'current' Vigilantes MC Victoria)

Warlocks (Geelong)

Original copper badge worn by 'Knackers' who was a founding member of the Angels.

The Angels formed in 1957 when they were one of only two clubs in Melbourne'—the Angels and the Vikings. Originally, the Angels and the Vikings all hung around together, meeting up at the beach at Williamstown or at Mama's Deli in Footscray or in one of the paddocks in Laverton where they would party with the local ladies.

The conservative 50s made way for the swinging 60s but the older generation, the 'law' and the press were not keen to embrace the new liberated lifestyles and sexual freedoms, and they clung to decades old ideals. The police attitudes were also stuck in the 50s. Some of the things club members got arrested for would be considered minor incidents today. Charges like 'obscene language', which landed some guys in court with fines. Another guy was arrested for going up to a girl in the park and asking if he could walk her home. He was trying his luck at picking her up, as many young fellas did at the time, but he ended up in court with his name splashed over the newspapers.

In the early days of the Angels, it was not unusual for a group of the boys to just hang out at Johnny's place. Most of the constabulary of the time saw all bike riders as troublemakers and any time motorcycles or leather jackets were seen, the police got out their charge sheets. Such was the fear of the 'Brando/bikie' image.

Knackers said, 'I had so many "Blueys" (infringement notices) I could have papered the walls with them! We were a bit wild but nothing like nowadays.'

At some stage the club started being referred to as a gang. That might have originated when trouble began between the Vikings and the Angels, and escalated into altercations. These were exaggerated by the newspapers, and eventually the Angels club was called the Angels Motorcycle Gang in the press, although they were always a 'club' to the members.

*

There are a number of perceived benefits for teenagers to be part of a club/gang.

A sense of belonging—Teens who feel they are misfits or are alienated from their families seek others who are like themselves. They look for like-minded groups where they will be accepted. They might look for a new 'family' to take care of them.

Protection—Members of a gang 'have each other's backs', so they usually hang out in groups to prevent rival gangs or anyone else from 'jumping them'.

Social interaction—Members spend time hanging out, getting into trouble and partying. A shared experience of music, drugs, alcohol, sex and fighting have appeal and create shared memories.

Excitement—Some like the thrill of doing something to see if they can get away with it. They enjoy the rush they get from pushing the boundaries or defying authority.

Money—Some gangs are money making industries. Some see clubs as a way to make a quick dollar dealing drugs, stealing and selling stolen goods, and trading weapons.

Although the Angels didn't consider themselves to be a gang at first, the members could relate to some of these 'benefits' of being in the club. One big difference was that the Angels, as a group, were never focused on business or financial dealings but that's not to say there were not members or friends who were involved in that kind of thing. Any of these financial arrangements were private ventures and not sanctioned by the club.

In the swinging 60s and 70s, drugs were easily available almost anywhere on the streets—even in sleepy old Williamstown. It was a working-class suburb and there was not a lot to do for teenagers. On Sundays, the streets were relatively empty, but the Angels could always find something to do—a place to hang out or go for a ride together.

Angels' membership card and patch.

top: Centre is Johnny Wilde (with the pointy-toed shoes).
bottom: Some of the boys on their bikes.

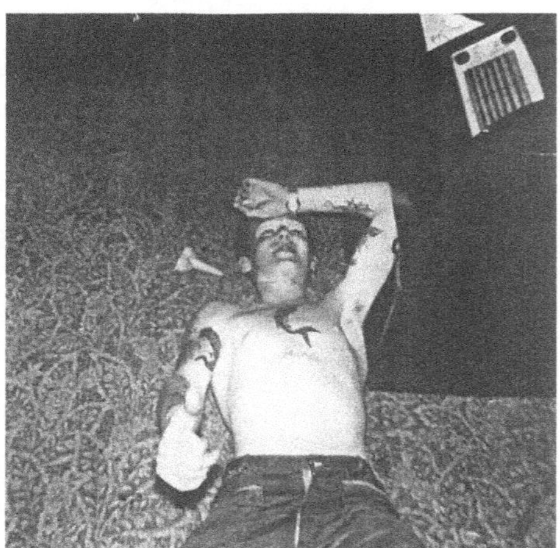

top left: Under the grandstand at Williamstown Racecourse.
top right: On the road.
bottom left: Having a drink in the paddocks of Truganina.
bottom right: Sleeping it off after a night on the booze.

The lure of the road and the smell of the leather was strong around Williamstown. In 1973, some fifteen- to eighteen-year-olds created their own gang and called themselves The Devil's Raiders. They walked around Williamstown in their leather jackets with a 'made-up' emblem on the back and acted tough, but most of them didn't even have a motorcycle! They had plenty of attitude but nobody took them seriously. Later down the track, when they eventually got bikes, some of the Devil's Raiders became the Critters.

Of course, the Angels or the Devil's Raiders weren't the first motorcycle clubs in Williamstown. The Williamstown Motorcycle Club had been established in 1930 by Len Bevis and his friends. Regular meetings were held in Len's workshop in Ferguson Street, Williamstown. Unfortunately, the club did not survive to the end of World War II as many of its members failed to return from their overseas service to 'King and Country'. The club reformed in 1996 to carry on the Williamstown tradition.

I'm still good mates with a lot of those blokes.

Abandoned Williamstown Racecourse where kids used to ride motorbikes by day and 'party' under the grandstand by night. The grandstand is long gone, leaving behind some rubble and stone steps. The site is now known as Altona Coastal Park and is a conservation area where Kororoit Creek runs into the sea. A lone palm tree marks the place where the Angels had so much fun.

CHAPTER 5

VIOLENT TIMES

My father was one of those men who sit in a room and you can feel it: the simmer, the sense of some unpredictable force that might, at any moment, break loose, and do something terrible.
— John Burnside

There seems to be an innate desire in young males to 'prove' themselves—to be an 'alpha male'. It happens in the animal kingdom and it is a human trait as well. The Angels were keen to prove themselves by racing their bikes, fighting or by 'getting the girl'. They also had a collective need to belong and a healthy disdain for authority. These things sometimes led to trouble.

Australia has a rich history of altercations between opposing groups—Aboriginal groups battled each other long before Europeans set foot here—often over women or turf. European settlers fought Indigenous Australians and slaughtered many of them for land. Convicts rebelled against authority and miners 'bucked the system' at Eureka Stockade with a rebellion.

No 'gang' is more famous in Australian history than bushranger, outlaw and national icon, Ned Kelly, and his gang. Ned identified himself as a larrikin when he wrote in the 'Jerilderie Letter' in 1879:

> The Queen must surely be proud of such heroic men as the police and Irish soldiers. As it takes eight or eleven of the biggest mud crushers in Melbourne to take one poor little half-starved larrikin to a watch house.[1]

The Angels considered themselves to be larrikins. We were the 'baby boomers' of the 40s, 50s and 60s—many of us were raised in homes where corporal punishment was the norm. 'Wait until your father gets home!' was a common threat and fathers would deal out punishment, usually in the form of a smack but sometimes it was a belting.

There was no equality for women. The man was the head of the household and he could do anything he pleased in 'his' home. Violence against women was prevalent and there was not much support for women who were beaten by their husbands. Society was of the opinion that the husband must have a good reason for being violent, and they made excuses for him: 'He was drunk', 'The wife must have upset him' or perhaps 'The war was to blame' for his violent outbursts. Regardless of excuses, women were victimised, often stuck in violent situations and their children suffered as well.

Society, at this time, labelled women who divorced as being of loose morals or 'failures'. Priests encouraged women to stay in violent marriages and told their female parishioners 'we all have burdens to bear'. The prevailing opinion was, 'You made your

1 Ned Kelly to Joe Byrne, 1879.

bed, now lay in it.' Just as my mum was told after she married the old man.

Children suffered violence at the hands of their parents. In my house, the old man used his fists with full force to discipline us and sometimes 'put the boot in' as well. I am sure I was not the only one in the club to be treated like that as a child.

Wife bashing and beating children was considered 'nobody else's business'. Police would seldom intervene between a husband and wife when answering a domestic disturbance call for help—in fact, they sometimes didn't answer the calls at all if they had previously been called out and the woman had withdrawn her complaint through fear or because she had nowhere to go.

It was not unusual to see a woman with a split lip or a black eye walking in our neighbourhood, and there was little to no social or legal support available for battered women and children.

Schools were no better and teachers were encouraged to physically discipline children until 2005, when the law was changed to stop the use of corporal punishment in schools in Victoria. In the 50s, 'Spare the rod and spoil the child' was a common saying, and common practice.

There was also a 'make a man of him' attitude by some fathers as they dealt out excessive violence towards children, unaware that they were teaching their children to use violence to solve problems in their adult lives. So, in those days, before corporal punishment was outlawed in schools, and when it was commonplace to be physically reprimanded in the homes, it was not unusual for young men and boys to use violence to work out issues. It was also common for brothers to have punch-ups and give each other bloody lips or even a broken bone now and then. There was usually no malice and such demonstrations of strength were encouraged by some fathers and seen as proof of manliness.

The 60s brought a focus on women's liberation and highlighted the need for support in local communities for battered wives. Women's refuges provided a safe haven for families and attitudes of women and towards women changed. Then the 70s brought the 'rights of the child' into focus and things started to change with more women's refuges being supported by governments throughout Australia. Change has been slow since then and tragedies still occur, but government and community attitudes continue to change to attempt to protect women and children. We are moving forward towards family safety but, sadly, we are not there yet.

Of course, not all family homes were places of excessive violence, but this account of the times is included to highlight that I was not the only child with a difficult home life and others in my circle had similar experiences. We learnt to protect ourselves and our circle of friends/family. The Angels, like other 'gangs' of the times, never took a backward step when challenged.

This Angel is 'owning' the traditional uniform of a black leather jacket, jeans, boots and the Brando sunglasses!

Angels hanging out with the locals and the ladies.

CHAPTER 6

READ ALL ABOUT IT!

If you don't read the newspaper, you're uninformed. If you read the newspaper, you're misinformed.
— Mark Twain

In the early 1900s, Melbourne had its fair share of gangs and larrikins. The following article, published in a Footscray newspaper in 1908, demonstrates both the desire to belong to a gang and the level of fear in the community, which led to victimisation by police.

"THE HEARTS AND ARROWS."[1]

A Footscray Push.

"These four are of a gang of youths known as the 'Hearts and Arrows.'" There were four lads, each about 17

1 Original clipping provided by Mrs Gibbons.

years of age, introduced at the Footscray (Victoria) court on Monday. They had been charged with stealing four eggs, and all denied the alleged offence.

The sergeant stated as a laugh went around the court, that the gang had been frightening the lives out of people. A constable said he saw the five lads sitting around a fire in a disused quarry. When they caught sight of him they bolted … One lad admitted that he was branded on the leg with a heart and an arrow, but all the push were not similarly tattooed. Three of them were fined, and the other was discharged.

"THE HEARTS AND ARROWS."

A Footscray Push.

"These four are of a gang of youths known as 'The Hearts and Arrows.'" Thus were four lads, each about 17 years of age, introduced at the Footscray (Victoria) court on Monday. They had been charged with stealing four eggs, and all denied the alleged offence.

The sergeant stated as a laugh went round the court, that the gang had been frightening the lives out of people. A constable said he saw five lads sitting round a fire in a disused quarry. When they caught sight of him they bolted. In a pot on the fire were four eggs. One lad admitted that he was branded on the leg with a heart and an arrow, but all the push were not similarly tattooed. Three of them were fined, and the other was discharged.

The youth rebellions of the 50s, 60s and 70s led to teens who dressed in the 'uniform' of sedition, choosing to rebel against society with their choice of clothing, music and lifestyle. They congregated with others who shared their contemporary values. They formed clubs or gangs of like-minded teens and society was afraid of this rebellion.

News stories of the time fuelled this fear and articles like this one served to promote hysteria, hatred and fear in the community. This led to victimisation by the police. There was an official government push to eliminate motorcycle clubs and the police supported this by responding with force.

This article which appeared in *The Truth* on 22 February 1962 demonstrates the level of panic fed by the media:

JUVENILE VIOLENCE[2]

> **Nothing can be done to cure the disease of juvenile delinquency until the nation admits that it is thinking about the peril nearly 20 years late ... Treatment and prevention of the worst delinquency could be much less difficult if the disease could be isolated and attended.**
>
> **But post-war delinquency the world over has become an invisible and acute medical sickness with strange and dreadful physical manifestations.**
>
> **As Mr. William Rogers—US Attorney-General until the now Kennedy administration—told me in Washington six years ago:**
>
> **"We have bred a young race of criminals far more vicious and dangerous than those in the age of Al Capone and Dillinger."**

The article went on to say that those opinions were based on an American study but that 'larrikin packs' had always been present in Australia. It went on to bemoan the fact that the age of the current gangs was getting lower and that was a concern.

The Truth newspaper had a reputation for being sensationalist and 'beating up' stories. Gangs in Australia at that time were nowhere near the likes of Dillinger and Capone

2 Dower, *Melbourne Truth*, 1962.

who were organised crime bosses. Most Australian 'delinquent' gangs of the time had no financial/business interests at all. The original Angels' only interests were sex, motorcycles, hot rods, alcohol and having a good time—with the occasional punch-up.

The 'punch-up' was a way to test courage and physical prowess. Males of many species fight for the right to mate or to rule. Men fought to prove themselves, to protect their people, their property and their pride. Of course, a big incentive was to 'mate' with females.

Tribalism plays a big part in all this and the tribe of Angels were no exception—fighting to test their prowess, protect their property and people, and to impress women. Apart from the innate 'nature' of men to test themselves against each other, there was also a very strong 'learned' element in fighting: boys learned what is was to be a man from their fathers, their male teachers and other role models.

POLICE TO BREAK UP PACKS —HUNT ORDERED[3]

> **Following street fighting in South Oakleigh last Saturday night between two gangs of young louts from the Footscray, Maidstone and Altona districts, orders have been given to special police squads to break up the gangs.**
>
> **The police plan to completely smash any attempt at further organised rioting and will curb the larrikins at every turn, locking them up and charging them whenever they step out of line.**
>
> **The gangs "fly" around in cars and on motorbikes and any traffic offences will come within the orbit of the police.**

3 *The Sun*, 1962.

The police or the newspapers called the Angels louts, but they considered themselves more a bunch of larrikins. The term *larrikin* was reported in an English dialect dictionary in 1905, referring to 'a mischievous or frolicsome youth' and a 'larrikin streak' has been prevalent in Australian culture for a very long time. Some people believe it arose as a reaction to corrupt authority during Australia's convict past or as a reaction to norms of society imposed by officials from England on Australians. The term was used to describe members of the street gangs that operated in Sydney during the late nineteenth and early twentieth centuries.

The idea of the larrikin 'diggers' during World War I, with their disregard for pomp, ceremony and authority while fighting fiercely and bravely for their brothers is celebrated as the quintessential Aussie identity. Aussie soldiers were considered to be hotheads who would never back down from a fight. The Angels identified with the larrikin tradition of disdain for authority and railed against conservative norms of 50s and 60s Australia, and they didn't back down from a fight either. They were happy to have opportunities to prove themselves in battle.

The Angels were also called an 'outlaw' gang with members from mainly working-class towns from Williamstown to Footscray, and were proud to be larrikins. An over-abundance of testosterone-charged youth and a feeling of 'brotherhood' meant that a member being slighted often lead to a punch-up. They had their own set of values and ideals of 'helping out a mate' and many a brawl began when one of the Angels got into a fight and his mates jumped in to help out. This larrikin attitude, combined with an understanding that each member must stand up for the other, was an integral part of the Angels' culture but it was small scale fighting by today's standards with small scale violence against other gangs or people who had wronged them.

Springvale Town Hall held a rock'n'roll dance on Saturday nights and we regularly rocked up there to listen to the music, drink beer and pick up some girls. Inevitably, some sharpies or mods would arrive and trouble would break out. Sharpies and mods were rival gangs in the 60s and 70s. They were both a natural enemy of bikers. Sharpies were mostly Melbourne based and always looking for a fight. Their name comes from the 'sharp' clothes they wore as a uniform—Levi baggy jeans, cardigans and t-shirts. The Angels much preferred their tight jeans, t-shirts and leathers. Gangs congregated in large numbers and gang rivalries were commonplace. Mods were also natural enemies of the sharpies. Mods had their origins in England and dressed much like the rock group The Beatles. They usually had long hair, unlike sharpies who had very short crewcuts and often a mullet (long at the back). Some mods rode motor scooters and we ridiculed them for their choice of ride. You could be sure that there would be trouble when a gang of sharpies or mods invaded our territory. It might be a grudge, a disrespectful word or maybe it involved a girl, any excuse, but fists would fly and eventually the police would be called to break it up. Many nights were spent in lockup nursing sore heads.

Peter 'Honda', so called because he rode a Honda, knocked around with the Red Barons in the 60s. He remembers:

> Mods would go for you if you were by yourself. One night I was riding down a lane in Melbourne and I looked up and saw a group of Mods spread across the road coming towards me. I thought I was gone. I revved up the bike, rode like hell with both my legs out the side of the bike and cut a path through their gang! They got out of the way and I rode home.

The Red Barons on a road trip. The Angels knocked around with them now and then. Photographs courtesy of Peter Kime.

FIGHTING ANGELS' FINED £75 TOTAL[4]

Youths were brawling and shouting amid a loud revving of motorcycles outside premises known as the Abongo Club, Ripponlea, on Sunday night, St Kilda Court was told yesterday.

Twelve youths in leather jackets, some of whom said they were known as "the Angels", were fined a total of £75 by Mr W. Murray, SM, and three Justices of the Peace, on offensive behaviour charges.

Two knives and a knuckleduster were found in a room where the youths had been. They denied any knowledge of them.

A witness who was helping at the Bongo Club said he had seen them there before and they caused no trouble. All the youths pleaded not guilty. Charges against four were dismissed while 12 others were fined a total of £75.

The Angels fought with other bikie gangs, to defend their honour but they were on friendly terms with some other clubs too. The brawls they had, however, were usually a 'one-on-one' fight rather than the practice of some other gangs who ambushed and jumped a single person. I was to have personal experience of that kind of attack later, in the 70s, when I walked around a corner in Altona shopping centre one day. Some guys jumped me and one guy hit me in the mouth with a metal crowbar, knocking out my teeth and fracturing my skull before he realised that I was not the person he was looking for.

'Oh. Sorry mate!' he said.

I was lucky not to be killed. Unfortunately, my teeth were not so lucky with all of them broken at the gums and the dentist was unable to save them. My mother cried at the loss of my teeth.

---

4 Original clipping provided by Mrs Gibbons.

She said they were the best teeth in the family. I spent some time in the hospital with a fractured skull too because of that case of mistaken identity.

Motorcycle clubs got a lot of bad press in the 60s and some of it was unwarranted by today's standards. Occasionally the Angels got blamed for things that other gangs did, like this article that appeared on 13 January 1962 on page 4 of *The Truth* newspaper with the headline:

> "THE WILD ONES" ON BEACHES[5]
>
> **Police Clash with Ghouls, Angels and Vikings**
>
> **Teenage Hoodlums—some carrying dangerous weapons—have stormed down the Mornington Peninsula in souped-up jalopies and motorcycles this holiday season and given local police their most torrid time in years.**
>
> **Police have seized knives, a metal bar and a powerful rifle; fought several pushes to a standstill and laid 50 charges ranging from larceny to drunken driving, offensive behaviour and indecent language.**

The Angels were no strangers to altercations and fights, as I said, but on this occasion, they were not even in the area.

The newspapers seemed to revel in demonising the Angels and exaggerated the facts with reports like this from *The Sun*:

> POLICE HALT "ANGELS" STREET PARTY[6]
>
> **Five carloads of police broke up a gang meeting of about 200 youths and girls of the "Angels" gang at Laverton**

---

5 Dower, *The Truth*, 1962.

6 *The Sun*, 1962.

> **late last night. Police described the scene when they arrived as "an orgy".**
>
> **Three fires had been lit in the middle of an unnamed road, off Dohertys Road, and youths were drinking around the fires, they said.**
>
> **Stacks of bottles and cans of beer lined the roadway.**
>
> **Almost 40 cars, including 11 "hot rods" and 37 motorcycles were parked nearby.**
>
> **Early today, after the gang left, police said they found dozens of motorcycle chains.**

According to one of the girls present, the truth was very different from the newspaper account. On that particular occasion, there were only one hundred people there, twenty or so bikes, one hot rod and about ten cars. Police simply issued unroadworthy infringements for some of the cars because the Angels weren't doing anything illegal.

*

The Angels were in the news far too often when they formed a guard of honour at the funerals of one of their own or of a biker from another club. The line of motorcycle riders would stretch far down the road, making visual representation of their mark of respect.

Peter Kime of the Red Barons remembered the funeral of an Angel, John St John:

> In the late 60s I rode, on and off, with a group in the Maidstone/West Footscray area called the Red Barons. They became loosely associated with the Angels because we were all in the same area.
>
> I still remember a lot of them but only by their nicknames. I only see one of the Barons now and

occasionally talk to Shorty, who was an Angel. I met Wildey a few times and he came around to look at a 52 Ford twin spinner I had for sale about twenty-five years ago. I used to go to the Kangaroo Rally in Ballarat until it was stopped, a lot of Angels and the Red Barons used to attend. Some of the Barons also ended up with the Hells Angels.

A few years ago, in '68 or '69, I caught up with Shorty at the funeral of one of the Angels. Shorty wanted an Indian (motorcycle) and had the hots for my 35 Chief. He was always after me to sell it to him. That never happened and I still have the Indian.

The day of the funeral, we all met up outside a flat in St Kilda and escorted the coffin to Fawkner Cemetery. There were about 200 bikes in the entourage.

That day, one of the Angels asked me if I could take a girl home to Maidstone after the funeral and of course I said 'yes'. She hopped on the back of the bike and off we went. We all stopped at a pub on the way home for a drink before I dropped her off. That girl ended up being my wife.

Funeral of John St John—Red Barons, Angels and others outside a St Kilda flat.

top: The Red Barons were a local club from Maidstone and Braybrook. Local clubs usually got along with each other pretty well. Curtesy of Peter Kime.

middle: The Red Barons on the road. Curtesy of Peter Kime.

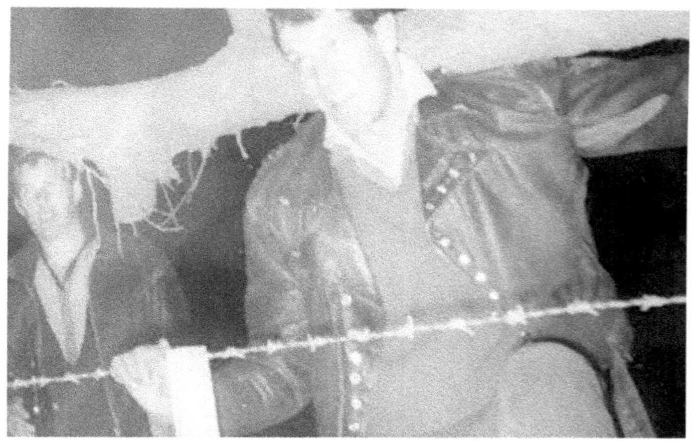

Knackers—collecting firewood for the barbecue at the old Williamstown Racecourse and hanging out under the abandoned grandstand.

Although the Angels got blamed for some things they didn't do, some of the guys did things they would be ashamed of now. There are bound to be 'dickheads' in and around any group and the Angels were no exception. There were people who hung around with the Angels who were not really part of the club and their behaviour was sometimes questionable. Those who committed serious indiscretions were handled 'behind closed doors' in the club and those who stepped over the mark were chastised by the other members. In the early days, five of the Angels were charged with attempted murder after the Vikings and Angels clashed in a Truganini paddock between Werribee and Laverton. Someone had a .22 rifle and shots were fired.

The *Altona Star* reported the following stories in 1962 and 1963:

DOUBLE SHOOTING[7]

Two Men Wounded Five Altona Youth Charged

In the City Court on Saturday last week, five Altona youths were charged with having wounded (name removed) 22, of Webb Street Altona, with intent to murder. They appeared before Mr R. Prowse SM and those charged were (names removed). Sergeant Swan said that at about 10.30 pm on Friday night the five accused went with other youths to a spot at the side of the road at Truganina where a party was in progress. The group was armed with a rifle and a fight started when they clashed with two gangs known as "the Angels" and "the Vikings". After some shots were fired a youth was hit in the back but was not seriously hurt. The youths were remanded to Sunshine Court next Friday and were each allowed bail of £100 with a similar surety.

---

7 Original clippings provided by Mrs Gibbons.

SHOT IN THE BACK

Five youths appeared in Sunshine Court charged with having wounded a 21-year-old Altona man with intent to murder. The man (name removed) said when giving evidence that he was shot in the back at a barbecue at Truganini about 8 miles from Altona, on the night of January 5th. (The victim), a truck driver, said that he went to Truganini at 9pm on Friday with a group of 20 youths and girls. They had a barbecue and drank liquor. At about 10pm a car came up with its headlights full on and facing towards them.

Someone called out, "It's the Altona boys" and (the victim) with several others from the barbecue approached the car.

"We knew there was a fight coming. We were 30 feet from the car when a rifle was fired. The headlights of the car were on us and I saw bullets hitting the ground at the feet of one of my friends. I turned and ran a pace or two. Bullets were whizzing past me and then I was hit and fell to the ground. I could feel the pain in my back."

He said he heard about 20 shots fired. He was later driven to Footscray Hospital. The victim said that at 5pm on Monday January 8th (name removed) in Blyth Street told him he was sorry about hitting him and said they had been after the Vikings. The Court were told that the Vikings were a gang of motorcycle boys. The victim said he was one of the bike boys and was at the barbecue with some of the Angels and some of the Vikings but he was not a member of either gang.

The victim said there had been a clash between the Altona boys and the Vikings at Lorne over Christmas and a rumour was around that the Altona boys were seeking revenge after having been beaten up. He added that he was not a fighter and had not been in trouble with the police. Five youths were remanded.

Johnny remembered:

> The shooting? That was just newspaper talk, really. There wasn't much to it. It didn't go anywhere anyway. I think they got community service.

Some articles were like comic book accounts: full of propaganda and with very emotive language. This account obviously came from a very biased source.

ANGELS ON RAMPAGE AGAIN[8]

> **During a social at the Williamstown Life Saving Club last Sunday night, about 25 members of the gang known to police as the Angels roared down on motorcycles and in cars and barged into the hall. The dance was being held to climax the annual life-saving carnival at Williamstown.**
>
> **As the Angels moved in and started their usual takeover activities, the life-savers went into action. The Angels stood up and challenged them, but their jeers turned into frightened yells of get out quick as the life-savers punched and bustled them out of the hall.**
>
> **The Angels gained a little more courage when one member of the gang produced a bike chain. He was knocked to the ground and they began their terrified flight. When the police arrived at the hall, the gang had fled. It was the first time the gang had been met by an equal number in a fair fight and is further proof that the gang are only to be feared when they outnumber their opponents or are attacking young girls or elderly people.**

The Angels often went to dances and functions—after all, that's where the girls were. The girls were attracted by the bikies and

8 Original clipping provided by Mrs Gibbons.

the bikies were attracted to the girls. The life-savers obviously stretched the truth to make themselves sound like heroes but even by their own account, the life-savers started the altercation. This resulting article was a total fabrication designed to defame the Angels who certainly did not attack the elderly or young girls.

MAD MOTORBIKE MOBS[9]

Mobs of youths on motorbikes from Altona, Newport and Williamstown have been causing concern to the residents of the Altona Migrant Hostel. The youth, known as the Angels and the Vikings race around the hostel roads on their bikes and use the bridge which leads to the Altona Sports Park, formally the Williamstown Racecourse.

Some time ago, the bridge was fenced off with high cyclone and barbed wire fence but the wire has been cut and pulled back allowing motorbikes to get through. The fence was erected by the Altona Shire Council to keep the hostel children out of the sports park and from climbing on the grandstand which no longer has any protective railings around the tiers and consequently is a grave danger to children.

Residents realise it would be difficult to keep the mobs out of the sports park. But we do not want them entering the

9 Original clipping provided by Mrs Gibbons.

> **park from the hostel. Apparently, their actions in the park as evidenced by the writing on the grandstand walls, leaves a lot to be desired and migrants are extremely anxious to protect their teenaged children and their daughters from these youths.**
>
> **However, some of the parents do not want the bridge closed off as it gives them access to the park and the beach. For showers and toilet facilities migrants have to leave their flats and walk to the public conveniences. Parents are afraid to let their daughters go alone.**
>
> **Recently Mrs Maguire of the hostel disturbed a mob of 20 youths waiting to accost the youth leader as he left the recreation hut. She asked them to leave the grounds and rang the police. After the youths had gone, she found a kosh approximately 15 inches in length which was of solid iron about 1 inch thick. She presumed this was to be used on the youth leader.**
>
> **This mob had threatened to beat him up because on a previous occasion he rang the police to have them removed from the hostel. Last Sunday morning Senator W Knight MLC, representing Williamstown Council and Senator W G Cresser, attended a meeting called by the hostel residents. Senator Knight said the trouble when you shift these gangs from one place, they move off elsewhere and cause trouble.**

It seems the Angels were blamed for graffiti without any evidence to connect them to it other than the fact they used the park and the grandstand for parties. The hostel parents, though, had good cause to worry about their daughters who were often keen to party in the park with the boys and snuck out after dark to join the fun.

ANGELS AND VIKINGS FIGHT AT OAKLEIGH[10]

Rival teenage gangs fought a pitched battle in Vera Street, South Oakleigh after crashing a girl's birthday party there late last Saturday night. Police said the gangs came from Footscray, Williamstown and Altona.

Car crank handles, bottles, boots and fists flew for half an hour when about 30 youths from the gangs known to police as the Vikings and Angels brawled in the street after a dispute over girls at the party.

(Name removed) 19 years, of West Footscray who admitted to police that he was an Angel was treated at the Alfred Hospital for head cuts after police led by Senior Constable R. Wetzlir of Brighton found him lying stunned and bleeding on the nature strip. It is thought his injuries were caused by a crank handle.

Residents said from the amount of broken glass and blood on the road and footpaths at least half a dozen other youths must be nursing other undisclosed injuries. Residents watching the fight from behind closed doors said the youths drove their cars up and down the street.

One onlooker said that one youth drove a car straight at another youth knocking him down but apparently not injuring him. The brawlers ran when police arrived. The police stopped the party.

Householders later hosed away broken glass, torn clothing and blood. Police alleged later that the two gangs whose members often rode motorcycles had caused trouble on peninsula beaches during the Christmas holidays. Supervised fight for gangs? Teenaged gang leaders should be put into a ring with boxing gloves for a supervised fair fight.

The Deputy Chief of the CIB, Chief Inspector H. McMennenin said, "This would go a long way towards stopping outbreaks of violence between rival gangs."

---

10 Original clipping provided by Mrs Gibbons.

> **He deplored inconvenience caused to householders in last Saturday night's brawl between the two teenaged gangs known to the police as the Vikings and the Angels.**

Fighting Franga on his Harley.

Attacks by rival gangs with knives or bike chains were not uncommon and, in the course of defending themselves, the Angels started to carry knives or chains. In the 70s, this was still the case as I had the misfortune to discover.

Springvale Rock was a rock'n'roll dance in a hall where we often went to listen to a band or two. One night, I was chatting up a girl and we were getting along pretty well when a guy came at me with a knife. I was unarmed and he stuck the knife into my hand. I managed to kick the knife out of his hand but, as it fell to the ground, it got stuck in my foot. My friends came to my aid and fists were flying. Then lots of others dived in and the whole thing ended in a big punch-up.

Knackers' son, Rod, recalled what his father told him about violent times and the Angels:

> Dad was an Angel—they called him 'Knackers'. Dad told us they camped and mucked around at 'Trucka-ninny'—it was his little joke for Truganini. He was good mates with 'Jack I' who said Dad could always be relied upon to 'have his back', but one time, someone must have played up and bullets were flying. Dad hid behind a tree to avoid being shot. Jack I wasn't so lucky and got shot in the back. Years later, when Jack I passed away and was cremated, the funeral parlour removed the bullet and gave the bullet to his son.

CHAPTER 7

ANGELS' CODE OF CONDUCT

Never fear quarrels but seek hazardous adventures.
— *The Three Musketeers* by Alexandre Dumas

Even though the Angels were raised in an era where it was the norm to use physical force, which they did against rival gangs, there was a code of conduct that governed members of the club. A code that they thought embodied attributes of fairness, honour, justice and inclusiveness. They would fight to support each other (loyalty); they would fight one-on-one (fairness); they would never sucker punch anyone (honour); they would protect themselves with weapons if they were attacked with weapons (justice); they would not 'gang up' on individuals (honour); anyone was welcome to join, regardless of ethnicity (inclusivity); and they never tried to 'move in' on any girl who was in a relationship with one of the brothers (honour).

Having found a place to belong, they fought to keep it and to maintain their lifestyle. They fought for the honour of their 'brothers' and to prove themselves. They were 'All for one and one for all' like The Musketeers.

It was not unusual for the police to use violence in the 50s, 60s and 70s. Police would pull us up and give us defect notices on our bikes and cars, and some would give us a beating after picking us up without any real cause.

Some of the Angels circa 1965. Just hanging out in the backyard.

In 1971, I was sitting in a car with some of the Angels in Deer Park. We were parked behind the shops in suburbia and waiting for one of the girls to meet up with us. She was a bit late and the guys started smoking dope and popping pills when a police car turned up. We waited. Then three more police cars came. They dragged some of us out of the car and belted us up a bit while one of the other blokes from the car yelled to the cop who was punching me, 'Leave him alone—he wasn't taking anything!' It was true and the sergeant must have believed him because he threw me the car keys and told me to drive the car to the police station, so I did. I was only sixteen at the time, and didn't have a licence!

Police brutality was rife and it was expected that those who were suspected of a transgression would get a beating at the hands of certain police during 'questioning'—even when the crime had not been of a violent nature. All of us were aware of cases where a pencil was laced through a suspect's fingers and a phonebook was slammed down on the hand, causing a broken finger or two. Tales were told of guys who had been beaten with a phone book around the head or body or even put in a metal cabinet and pushed down stairs by police trying to get a confession from a suspect. When guys got treated like that, is it any wonder they had no respect for the 'force'—in fact, the police were hated. It wasn't until the report of the 'Board of Inquiry into Allegations against Members of the Victoria Police Force' in 1978 that a light was shone on this kind of aggressive illegal behaviour by some of the police force. After this report was made public, we had a higher expectation of relative safety when we were in the hands of the police.

There were some good coppers who would just give us a verbal 'kick in the arse' and let us go for minor offences like drinking in public, displays of public affection (making out in the park) or swearing. One Footscray lad was unlucky to be caught by a not so good copper and was fined five pounds or six weeks in jail for using foul language in a billiard hall.

There was one particular Newport and Williamstown policeman who was always fair. We had respect for him because he would talk things out and was never violent towards us. We called that particular 'copper' Constable Swallow, because of the little tattoo he had on his arm. Constable Swallow remembers his dealings with the Angels:

> My first encounter with the Angels was as a twelve- or thirteen-year-old when I went with an older relative to a swimming hole that the Angels frequented. It was near Overnewton Road in Keilor, near the old bridge and we used to swing on a rope and drop into the river. I thought they were a nice sort of people.
>
> Later, when I joined the police force, I knew the Angels and they weren't vicious, not like the bike gangs now. They were just a bunch of young bucks—free-spirited boys who would get together down by the Pines in Altona and have a barbecue. There weren't any drugs like there are now and they were reasonably respectful towards us. A grudging respect, I would say. They didn't cause a lot of trouble. Most of the other local police said the same about them. If they did get into a bit of trouble, some police members would drive them down to Cobbledicks Ford and let them out of the car. They would be told to walk back and cool off. We didn't want to take them to court and have it on their record, so we did that instead.

When they were dropped off at Cobbledicks Ford, the young offenders did not appreciate that the police were trying to do a 'good turn' for them.

One group saw it as a kind of a game or challenge and set out to beat the police car back home. They pinched a farmer's car and rode back in style. They left the car parked on the street where the farmer could get it back and made jokes, laughed and congratulated themselves for beating the coppers back home.

AN ANGEL AND HIS BIKE

105 mph AN
GIRL ON THE
PILLION

COURT TOLD

One of our Footscray larrikins was clocked doing 105 miles per hour riding his Norton Mark11 (which he ordered from the US for £564) down the Nepean Highway, with his girlfriend riding pillion passenger. The police took off after him with their siren wailing but they couldn't catch him.

The next day, he went to the Cheltenham Police Station and said, 'I believe you want me. I don't know what got into me? I couldn't hear the police siren because of the helmet over my ears!'

A likely story!

He appeared in court and was fined fifty pounds for speeding and three pounds for driving without a licence but asked the judge if he could pay the fine off over time. The judge did not agree. 'This is not a time payment situation!' he said, though he still gave the rider three months to pay. Outside the court, the young offender said he rode with the Angels—a black leather-jacketed, high power motorcycle group.

Knackers laughed at this because one requirement of joining the Angels was to ride at *least one hundred miles per hour.*

*

Wildey was often a stabilising factor and his guidance kept many a young fella out of trouble. His door was always open for blokes seeking advice. One youngster was tempted by an offer from some acquaintances to drive a getaway car during a robbery. The deal sounded very lucrative and the young bloke thought he wouldn't be participating in the robbery by just driving the car. Wildey put him straight and convinced him that it would not be a good idea to be involved in any way. That robbery went ahead without the young bloke. The robbers got caught and each was sentenced to seven years jail.

Wildey's words of wisdom … 'Don't go with those dickheads. You'll end up in the shit.' This was repeated many times to many young blokes, including myself. He was a true leader in the group and tried to lead his brothers away from criminal behaviours that would end up in jail time, or worse.

left: Johnny Wilde (right) with David Gibbons (left) at his mum's place in Newport.

right: Two Angels having a beer with a furry friend.

Photos fade with memories. These faded photos of the Angels socialising are included to jog and preserve memories of a time gone by.

CHAPTER 8

A LITTLE ANGEL —60s AND 70s

I believe that I understand gangs better than others because they are formed out of necessity. They're formed by people to keep from being oppressed.
— Jack Bowman

I had tagged along with Johnny to the Angels' meetings from the time I was about ten years old and I finally felt like I belonged somewhere. I saw the bikies as a band of brothers who looked out for each other.

They had meetings in pubs or at their homes and they were just blokes on bikes—no colours (big badges or names) or anything. Just blokes who loved riding and working on bikes, formed a club and supported each other like brothers.

Johnny owned the old house next door to his house and an old laundry out the back. The laundry made a good workshop but an even better unofficial club house and party house for the Angels. There was a barrel of beer on tap with music playing The Beatles, Credence, The Stones and rock'n'roll nonstop.

There was a steady flow of girls, attracted by the image, and the excitement of being part of the club. Some with a genuine interest in the bikes and bikies but others who were craving a place to belong—just like me at age ten, eleven, twelve.

I learnt a lot about life in that house. It was a real eye-opener. I watched the comings and goings, and the girls that hung around, and I wished I was part of it, but that came later. If the party was not suitable for me, Johnny Honda, Phillip C. and other guys used to put me in a helmet and lift me onto the back of their bikes when they needed to get rid of this little kid with wide eyes and attitude. I loved it.

I also got a ride when the guys went to visit other members at their homes. I tagged along and was thrilled to be riding on the back of a motorcycle as 'part of the gang'. When one of the members retired, he handed his colours (from another club) onto me and I was honoured by this very magnanimous gesture. Colours are not supposed to be transferable but for me, he made an exception.

I used to stay with Johnny and Marion a few nights a week and then go home where I shared the corrugated iron shed in our backyard with my brothers. Glenn, Dale and I slept in bunk beds and a single. One day, the local constable came looking for a friend of ours who wasn't there at the time. He saw the shed and said, 'Do you boys sleep in there?' and we answered, 'Yes, that's our bedroom.' He just shook his head. It was pretty bad.

My first job was as an apprentice butcher when I was fourteen. After I got my first pay, I went out and bought ice-creams, lollies, soft drinks—all the things we didn't get at home.

Of course, my brothers found my stash of goodies and helped themselves, too.

I also bought a pair of Wrangler jeans and a jacket and went to Johnny's place where the Angels promptly rolled me in the dirt because they thought I looked too neat.

That job was short-lived and I started work as an apprentice jockey at Cakebread's Stables in Gordon Street, Footscray. I used to muck out the stables and exercise the horses. They were nasty beasts that would deliberately kick or bite at every opportunity. I loved it though. Unfortunately, I grew too big to be a jockey and that job came to an end.

I bought my first road bike when I was fourteen, too. It was a 250 BSA. I got it from a man in Challis Street in Newport and it leaked more oil than it used. I had to carry a toolbox in my pockets to keep it going but it was all mine!

In 1972, when I was just turned seventeen, I went to get a job at Eatmore Poultry where Angel Gibbo and his wife, Margie, worked. They didn't have a job for me inside but David, the boss, said to me, 'Can you drive?' and of course I said yes. So, he sent me out with Gibbo to learn the route in a small van used to deliver the chickens.

After a couple of weeks, the boss came and said they were very happy with my work but they wanted me to drive a big truck and he had organised, with a police officer he knew, for me to go to the police station and get my truck licence. What he didn't know was that I didn't even have a car licence! I only had a motorbike licence! I had to resign that day. I didn't want to get done for driving without a licence.

At seventeen, I went to work as an apprentice mechanic at a few different places including Eastcoast Transport. On my first day there, the foreman asked me if I could drive. Again, I said,

'Yes, I can drive.' There was a 'White' prime mover in the yard and the foreman said, 'Bring that truck inside.' I got in, put it in gear, took my foot off the clutch and went straight through the wire fence. The truck had no brakes. The boss went ballistic, not at me, but at the foreman for letting me drive a truck. I wasn't old enough to have a car licence.

Glenn and I moved out of the old shed and into an old bond wood caravan that my family bought to use for holidays. It was pretty rustic but it had two double beds—one at each end—and Glenn and I shared that. It was much better than the old doorless tin shed.

We often 'entertained' in that caravan. One morning the old man came in and shook the bundle curled up in Glenn's bed only to be confronted by a groggy, dishevelled, young girl. I hadn't seen the old man flustered before, but he was shocked, and went to get Mum so she could deal with the naked girl in Glenn's bed.

*

Although I wasn't sleeping at Johnny's house then, I still continued to hang around his place and lots of other guys gravitated to the group.

There were some real characters in the club. People who were really entertaining for this impressionable kid and other characters I admired greatly. We all had nicknames. I was nicknamed Crazy because I was a little kid who would try anything—especially when they told me I couldn't do it.

Another 'crazy' bloke was Chicken Man. Memories of the Sunbury Rock Festival flood back when I think of him. The festival was an annual sex, drugs and rock music festival held on a 620-acre private farm between Sunbury and Diggers Rest in Victoria over the Australia Day long weekend from 1972 to 1975. People packed into the area to camp in tents or in their cars and watched Chain, Billy Thorpe and the Aztecs, Max Merritt & The Meteors, and many other pop and rock performers.

Sunbury was an orgy of sex, drugs and rock'n'roll with near-naked men and women letting it all hang out. It was a wild old time and Chicken Man was one of the wildest. After some serious substance abuse, Chicken Man paraded around the festival wearing only a baby's nappy. He managed to make the news that night in a full-frontal shot that raised a few conservative eyebrows and set worried parents' minds to wondering what their children were up to at Sunbury on that hot summer's weekend.

Chicken Man doesn't remember much of what he did on that wild weekend, but here is what came to his mind:

> Oh Sunbury? Oh NO! (laughs)
>
> I found a sweetie and fell in lust. The coppers threatened to charge me with carnal knowledge but instead they put me in a 44-gallon drum and rolled me down the banks of the creek. The drum went in the water and I was floating in the creek and the coppers were laughing and laughing while I was sinking. Bastards.
>
> We had a keg of beer hidden in a 44-gallon drum of 'water'. There was water at the top but you could remove the top part to get at the beer. It was all harmless fun. We didn't destroy other people's property or anything. No tagging or anything either. It was good fun.

Johnny Wilde's memories of Sunbury add a little more to the picture:

> Sunbury? Oh crikey! Alcohol was banned there, but we had a 44-gallon drum we cut the bottom off and put an 18-gallon keg inside it—it just fitted in nicely. We welded the top back and put water in it. When the man on the gate was suspicious and asked what was in the drum, we told him, 'Water. We can't drink that river crap. We'd get sick! Turn on the tap!' Of course, when he did, we had fixed it so that water came out. We had our own marquis at Sunbury—a tent set up for the Angels and for freeloading coppers. We'd say, 'Do you want a beer?' and they said, 'Oh Yeah!' and they had a drink with us.

By this time, I was seventeen years old and had a girlfriend, Leanne, who was a nurse at Williamstown Hospital. Her parents had high hopes she would marry a doctor, so they were not too keen to let their daughter hang around with a motorbike rider of ill repute. On the weekend of the Sunbury Festival, she told her parents that she was going to the festival with a group of her friends. Of course, we arranged to meet there and stay in my tent. Under that canvas tent we cemented a relationship that would last more than thirty years.

An integral part of the gang was Sheepy. Like Chicken Man, he was a real character who had a heart of gold but his looks were very deceiving. Although his demeaner was extremely scary, he was one of the most decent guys I knew.

His mother was oblivious to the image he portrayed and the way he looked. She didn't see the tough guy image and she used to tell him that he was 'hanging around with thugs'.

He was hanging around with me and she said these things while I was sitting right there in her lounge chair in front of her. Sheepy looked more of a thug than I did, but she couldn't see it.

Image courtesy of Hedon Productions.

Sheepy's scary bikie look got him his five minutes of fame when he and some of the other guys were asked to make an appearance in an ABC TV show called *Bellbird.* This led to an appearance on the big screen.

Sheepy and some of the other guys rode their bikes from Melbourne to Sydney to appear in the 1974 movie *Stone.* They were extras in the film who lent some authenticity to the movie. *Stone* is a 1974 Australian biker film about police officer Stone who goes undercover with the Gravediggers outlaw motorcycle gang to find out who is murdering their members.

Some people believe *Stone* became a timeless Australian cult film, but we didn't rate it much. It was just a bit of fun.

Another film the Angels participated in making was *Petersen* (1974) which was filmed, in part, in St Kilda and starred Australian actor and international heartthrob, Jack Thompson.

> *Petersen* was a box office success and received wide distribution in the UK and US under the title *Jock Petersen. Petersen* is first and foremost a sobering critique of Australian life in the early 1970s. *Petersen* is considered one of the better social dramas from the early years of the Australian film revival. Stanley Kubrick praised the film on its release, particularly Burstall's direction and Jack Thompson's lead performance.[1]

---

1 Kuipers, 'Petersen (1974)'.

Wildey was given a fist full of money for the Angels' part in the movie and he didn't know what to do with it. He thought about sharing it between the guys who had appeared in the film but he settled on sharing it among the whole group with a big party that lasted three days. The food was incredible and set out on a table in the workshop were prawns, crayfish and chicken with salads and beer, and every type of spirits you could imagine. Chicken Man was shit-faced the whole time. He even tried to climb into the bin to get the remains of the crayfish the next day.

So many characters hung around with the Angels. All of them had an influence on me. Ray, Jeff and Tiny were the muscle brigade and each were incredibly strong.

Ray once lifted a motorbike above his head to show how strong he was. There may have been a bit of alcohol involved and a lot of cheering on.

Jeff got his motorbike down the sideway of a house and didn't have space to turn it around so he picked it up and pivoted around so he could ride it out.

Tiny helped Leanne and I move into a caravan behind my new in-law's house. We had gotten married and were having a baby, so we wanted to move the van so that it faced the right direction. There was a few of us trying to work out how to move it when out came Tiny. He stood tall and huge. He summed up the situation and his body language said, 'Out of the way!' Tiny lifted that 21-foot caravan and pulled it around sideways, all on his own.

Those guys were amazingly strong and really good blokes. They would do anything to help out a mate.

Another 'brother' was Fighting Franga, who was always looking for trouble, and he often found it. 'Bloody hell. What's Franga doing now!' was a frequent moan.

There were lots of drugs and booze around in the 70s, but Franga took it to a new level. He would take any substance known to man—even if he didn't have a clue what it was. This got him into lots of trouble and dragged the other brothers into it as well. If there was a punch-up, you could be pretty sure that Franga had something to do with it and the other Angels always helped him out. Even when he was wrong.

From time to time, while under the influence of grog, I managed to get myself into a bit of trouble and Franga helped me out.

One Saturday afternoon on the way out of the MCG (Melbourne Cricket Grounds) after watching the Bulldogs play, Franga, Pyke and I passed a group of Hare Krishna guys all dressed in orange robes and dancing about. They had set up a stall to sell their cards and flowers, and they got up really close and personal when you least expected it.

As I was walking past, one of the Krishna blokes came and tried to pin a flower on my white shirt but the pin missed its mark and stuck into my chest. Without thinking too much about it, I let fly with a fist and before I knew what had happened, Hare Krishna blokes came from everywhere and jumped on me. Franga and Pyke joined in and there was a big brawl. A crowd gathered and, sick of being harassed by the Hare Krishna, the crowd got behind us and cheered us on. The police, however, were not impressed.

I ended up in court before a judge, who said, 'What were you doing fighting Hare Krishnas? They are supposed to be peace-loving and pretty harmless.'

'Well, I don't agree with that. Look what they did to my face,' I said as I showed the judge a photo of my bloodied, mangled features.

As the Krishnas didn't appear in court, the judge dismissed the charges and I went to the pub for a celebration drink with Franga.

*

The real larrikin of our group was Baby Face. One hot summer day he was high on substances and beer at Williamstown Beach when he decided to climb onto the roof of the kiosk.

The boys in blue arrived and told him to get down but the cheeky kid refused. A crowd gathered and egged him on while he taunted the police with hands on the hips and wiggling his bum.

One policeman tried climbing up to catch him but the copper fell backwards onto the pavement to the sounds of laughter from the assembled crowd. Baby Face, enjoying the attention and feeling the call of nature, decided to add insult to injury and peed on the fallen copper, which delighted the crowd even more.

The youngest policeman climbed onto the roof to get the little villain. He dragged him down onto the footpath and rubbed his face in the wet uniform, then bundled Baby Face into the paddy wagon to take him to the lock-up. There he got a beating followed by a drenching from the fire hose in a cell.

A night in lock-up followed by a court appearance was the price he paid for this larrikin behaviour.

I first met Bowie Lynch when he rode a motorcycle to my house. He had the Marlon Brando jacket and the bikie look, and I thought he was pretty cool. My big sister, Pam, must have thought so too because she ended up marrying him.

Bowie was a good guy to me. He was a local Williamstown boy and worked with the old man driving trucks. He earned the respect of the old man for his work ethic and that was no mean feat.

Sometimes he took me in the cab with him when he was delivering frozen goods all over Victoria. I got to know him and looked up to him, so I was very happy when he married my sister and they had three kids together.

Bowie hung around with the Angels and loved bikes like I did. He was part of our close-knit group and therefore part of both my families. Unfortunately, his marriage to my sister didn't last and years later, even more unfortunately, Bowie lost his life when a neighbour, hyped up on drugs and alcohol, went crazy and attacked him as he sat on his front porch in a wheelchair. The attack was totally unprovoked, and the neighbour was out of his mind when he murdered Bowie with a kitchen knife. It was a tragic case of Bowie being in the wrong place at the wrong time.

Serge was from an Italian family and very proud of his jet-black Elvis style hair with its swept back sides coated in Brylcreem. Most of the guys had a bit of an Elvis look but Serge really mastered it. The others teased him for being a poser because he would ride along beside a bus and, if there were women in the bus, Serge would do a wheel stand (riding along on the back wheel with the front wheel in the air) to show off to the girls. Serge was a nice, decent bloke with a definite eye for the ladies.

Our resident 'tea-leaf' was DP. He had an eye for an unguarded item left in temptation's way and he helped himself whenever and wherever he could. In fact, he took anything that wasn't bolted down.

One night, he talked some of us into removing an old Ford 32 roadster body that was rusting in a farmyard. You have never seen a bigger bunch of dills pinching something in your life. We were full of beer as we climbed over the barbed wire fence and the four of us, laughing and staggering, carried the carcass of that old car to the fence where we had trouble hoisting it over.

The more we tried, the more we laughed and fell about. It's a wonder we didn't get crushed by that rust bucket but, somehow, we managed to get it over the fence and tow it away. Chicken Man remembers the incident like this:

> DP had a hot rod that was painted metal flake orange that we were taking to Narrandera for a 'hot rod run' but a car ran up the butt of the hot rod, so he needed a new body. He asked me to help him pick up one he found on an old farm, so I said, 'Okay. When?' He said, 'Midnight tomorrow night.' Well DP must have had pretty good vision because that car was a long way from the fence—it was like trying to find a pimple on an elephant's arse. There was no light as we headed to the hayshed across a paddock. There was no moon and it was pitch black.
>
> When we got to the hayshed the old car body wasn't at the front. It was jammed in behind a trailer up against a wall near a second car. Well there was a lot of noise of steel scratching and scaping while we tried to get it out and carry it to the fence. We were running across the paddock with the car—one of us on each corner. We got it over the fence and threw it on the back of the ute and we bolted.
>
> We drove a few miles down the road and then put a tarp over it. We were going to go down the quiet streets but decided to go down the main street at three o'clock in the morning. We were so pissed we thought that would be less suspicious—a ute with a tarp over the back driving down the main street at 3am. Drunken idiots!

That old car body was turned into a beautiful hot rod, and became someone's pride and joy.

Last but not the least of my Angel mates was Meat—so named because of his enormous appendage and his way with the ladies. Enough said.

Hot rod similar to the one salvaged from the farmyard.

top: Gibbo and his ride at Johnny's family home.

bottom: The Angels gather outside Mama's Milk Bar on the corner of Eleanor and Barkly Streets, Footscray.

CHAPTER 9

PARTYING

Sometimes our knight in shining armor turns out to be a biker in dirty leathers.
— Anonymous

As opportunistic blokes, we were always on the lookout for available women, and women were attracted to the image. There was a steady stream of girls who came to the house to party and a couple of 'runaways' who needed a place to crash would sleep in Wildey's workshop or at one of the other guys' houses.

Some girls came and coupled exclusively with one of the boys but others made themselves available to all. One of the girls used to sneak out of her bedroom window when a motorbike pulled up outside her house. She would be on the back of that bike and away before her parents even knew she had gone.

A lot of the guys were in relationships. The couples would go to house parties or to the old Williamstown Racecourse site in Altona or to Truganina Reserve near the old cemetery and hang out down there. We drank, ate a barbecue, had sex and talked shit. The police didn't really worry about us being at the abandoned Williamstown Racecourse and we didn't cause any trouble riding on the old dirt tracks or sitting around campfires.

There was not much else to do around Williamstown, Altona and Laverton. They were working class areas and people didn't go out much in the evening. There was a very limited choice for eating out or even for takeaway as the only places to choose from in Williamstown were a Chinese café on Nelson Place and a fish and chip shop. Fleet Wings Café was a service station in Laverton that stayed open late, and there was just one place in Altona—the fish and chip shop. The only real café to hang out at was Sam's Coffee Pot on the junction of Sommerville Road, Roberts Street and Geelong Road, opposite the 'Sign of the Flying Red Horse'—the Mobil Service Station. Sam's was where working people called in for lunch and where, at night, all the cool kids went and it was a regular haunt of the Angels.

Sam's Coffee Pot in West Footscray circa 1960.

Inside Sam's Coffee Pot—the only hamburger joint 'hangout' just west of Footscray.

George of Werribee remembers Sam's and the Angels:

> I used to knock around in Werribee with a couple of the Angels. I was only a kid and they used to pop me on the back of their bikes and ride around the streets. One of the boys was Kenny who had an old Bellaire Chev—big enough to land a helicopter on! A real 'Yank tank'. A mate said to me that we never had a diner like they had in America and I said, 'We had Sam's Coffee Pot!' That was the place to be.

Another hangout for the Angels was on the corner of Eleanor Street and Barkly Street in Footscray—Big Mama's. Big Mama (Lucy/Lucrecia) made hamburgers and milkshakes and the jukebox was a big drawcard for young people and other bikies in the area—not just the Angels.

Inside Big Mama's (Big Mama seated back left) at her milk bar on the corner of Eleanor and Barkly Streets, Footscray. Her son Leon is standing in the background on the right.

Mama's son Leon has fond memories of the Angels who frequented his mother's shop and recalled:

> I remember the Angels would always come into our delicatessen and café. I remember there was a ritual for inductees with their jackets—they had to drop the leather jackets on the floor and everyone would stomp on them to dirty them up. They did that in our shop.
>
> One day my brother Andy came home all bruised and bleeding. We loved dim sims and Andy had gone to Jimmy Wong's to get some when he got jumped and bashed. When Mama saw him, she was waving her arms around and crying.
>
> There was a group of Angels sitting at a table and one of them said to my brother, 'That's it! Come with us.'

> And they went and smashed the crap out of the ones who beat up Andy.
>
> The Angels ran up a 'tab' at the shop. Years later, Mama was sitting in the Commercial Hotel in Benalla and Johnny Wilde walked in. He came over and hugged her, 'Mama!' he said, 'I still owe you money.' Mama told him not to worry about it, but he gave her twenty dollars or so, to more than cover the tab.

The Red Barons hung around Mama's where they had a regular booth at the back of the shop. One of the Barons had a girlfriend who arrived very shaken and upset. She had walked past the Italian Club and some pretty nasty comments had been levelled in her direction. Some very bad stuff that left her shaking. A day later a copper came to see the Barons, 'Do you know anything about what happened at the Italian Club last night?' he asked. Of course, the Barons all shook their heads or looked at the floor or suddenly found something very interesting to stare at on the wall. No. They knew nothing. The constable went on, 'Last night a half dozen young blokes in leather jackets smashed up the place and broke a few heads and cleaned them up. You wouldn't know anything about that? Hmm,' he said with his chin to his chest and eyes up, scanning the room, 'hmmm.'

The Red Barons, like the Angels, stood up for their own.

The Angels spent a lot of time just hanging out together and sometimes the Barons or the Vikings joined us. We drank, ate a barbecue, chased the girls and sometimes we caught them, or they caught us—I'm not quite sure which. Some guys would take the girls down to 'Lovers Lane' and make the car rock. It was all good fun.

Partying with the ladies, indoors and outdoors, circa 1964. The girls were attracted to the bikies and the sense of freedom and rebellion that came from riding with a motorcycle gang. A few girls had their own motorcycles and some rode pillion, but all liked the barbecues, the bonfires and the parties.

Having a drink under the grandstand.

Night riding with the girls, circa 1964. Compulsory wearing of helmets did not come into law until 1973–74.

Angels—socialising with the ladies.

Hydie was a local police constable who remembers the Angels well:

> We used to get a call from one of the neighbours across from The Pines in Altona, complaining about the noise or just because there was a big group there. Four of us in a car would go and check it out and there might be up to one hundred kids there but there was never any trouble. If we had to speak to them, they just did what we told them. They were 'knock-about blokes'—just good fellas. Of course, some people were scared of them because of the way they dressed and because they were in a group, but really, young people express themselves and old people don't like that.

Just chilling with a mate in the backyard at Johnny's place.

Of course, not all the boys were as respectful of the police as the boys in blue thought. While the police were rounding up some of the gang, a couple of them were peeing in the coppers' petrol tanks.

Around that time, some of us would also go to the old ammunition reserve, Truganina, in Altona and ride our bikes or drink in the bunkers there and make out with the girls. Sometimes we got chased out by the caretaker and we would jump on our bikes and speed off down the track near the creek. Other 'party paddocks' were raided by the police, as this small news item in a newspaper indicates:

RAID ON GANG'S PARTY[1]

In raids on two suburbs last night, police arrested eight young people including a 15-year-old girl.

They broke up a drinking party by the "Angels" gang on the open land behind the Royal Park Psychiatric Hospital.

Police said the members of the gang from Williamstown, Footscray and Spotswood arrived at the spot about 9pm.

Police took possession of several motorcycle chains and a .22 rifle.

Three youths were questioned. Two will be proceeded against on summons.

When we weren't partying with the girls, we often just hung out together in pairs or smaller groups. Sometimes we camped out and went rabbiting.

One warm summer's night, Franga and I went to his brother's dairy farm in Druin—a Victorian country town about

1 Original clipping provided by Mrs Gibbons.

an hour and a half east of Melbourne. As the sun set, we grabbed our rifles and set out spotlighting to get some rabbits for dinner.

We were driving through the paddock in Franga's XY Falcon, when 'Splash!' We found ourselves in a green slime-covered, wastewater channel. Cow shit and slime from the milking shed seeped in through the doors and was rising rapidly towards the windows. We were literally in deep shit.

I climbed through a window, onto the roof and jumped to the bank. Franga climbed out the driver's side window and fell straight into the putrid waters. He emerged like the Creature from the Black Lagoon with slime dripping from his ears. I laughed and laughed.

'Shut up you fuckin' bastard!' Franga yelled as he stripped off all his clothes and left them on the ground next to the nearly submerged car.

I couldn't stop laughing as we walked back to the farmhouse in search of some help to get the car out, have a shower and put on some clean clothes.

We decided to take a shortcut and climb the wire fence that separated us from the house. When we reached the fence, I put my hand on the wooden post and jumped over the fence. Franga, in the nude, cocked his leg over the fence and let out a bloodcurdling scream. It was an electric fence to keep the cattle in the paddock and Franga's tackle had dangled on the wire.

The next day as we drove home, Franga was very quiet, and his eyes were wild and staring. I was still stifling a laugh.

David aged twenty-one in 1976.

CHAPTER 10

BOOZE, DRUGS AND ROCK'N'ROLL

Childhood is like being drunk. Everyone remembers what you did but you.
— Anonymous

Alcohol has always played a central role in white Australian culture. Australia's reputation for heavy drinking has its roots in British colonisation, in the Gold Rush era of the mid-1850s, and partly in bushman culture.

Male bonding—and mateship developed 'over a beer'—led to two drinking practices which persist to this day. The practice of 'shouting' is the term used when each man takes a turn to buy the others in the group a drink, making drinking a group activity. The Aussie tradition of binge drinking known as 'the six o'clock swill' was common practice in the days when hotels closed at 6pm. As closing time drew near, men crowded against the counter, four or five deep, the ones at the back calling over the heads of those at the bar. They jostled for positions and shouted and swore in an attempt to be served before closing time.

During these times hotels were segregated with only men (usually white males) able to drink in the bar while women were admitted to the Ladies' Lounge. Drinking was a way for men to bond with each other and share a camaraderie without the presence of women to moderate their behaviour.

In the 60s, there was a shift in this culture when hotels became places of entertainment and men and women began to socialise together in hotels where music was provided.

The Tarmac in Laverton was the local pub that showcased bands like Rose Tattoo and Lobby Lloyd where we drank, socialised and picked up women. The concentration of large numbers of young people in a crowded bar and alcohol combined with loud music created problems.

Poster advertising coming attractions at the local Tarmac Hotel, September 1977. The line-up featured Angry Anderson, vocals; Peter Wells, slide guitar; Michael Cocks, guitar; Ian Rilen, bass; and Dallas Royall, drums.

'Bouncers' were employed to manage rowdy behaviour and break up fights but they were often thugs—looking for trouble themselves and they became part of the problem. Many a small skirmish was escalated by the intervention of bouncers in the carpark. The next week an Angels' delegation would front up to seek revenge for a mate who had been set upon.

Local teenagers flocked there to party and drink, and couples engaged openly in various forms of physical intimacy. My sister worked behind the bar, so I had no trouble getting in even when I was underage.

At Wildey's place, there was always Stone's Green Ginger Wine and plenty of beer in the Angels' house in the 60s and, later in the 70s, a variety of drugs were on offer, too.

'Physical intimacy' was not an uncommon sight in the house. One time, I saw one of the girls who was obviously not in any fit state to make any choices. I knew her from around the neighbourhood and I knew her parents. Maybe she had taken something that, combined with the drinks she had, made her out of control—so much so that she couldn't stand up and couldn't even speak. I bundled her into my car and drove her home to keep her out of harm's way. I was no saint, but I didn't want anything to happen to her when she couldn't be responsible for her actions. She was very vulnerable and everyone was pretty wasted. I helped her to the door and rang the doorbell. Her parents didn't show any gratitude though and blamed me for her state—I was still perceived as an 'evil bikie'.

That was the perception then as it is now, but we were not evil. We were just boys who had a good time. There was a good side to all the blokes, although we did get into a bit of trouble while looking out for each other.

One of the girls remembered her time as part of the club very fondly:

> I really loved the camping out in the paddocks—not *all night* mind you—but it was fun. All the boys had trades and good jobs—they were good people.

There was a news program on Sunday nights and once they did a story about the paddock where we had our parties. They collected all the beer cans and made a big pile and tried to make out like we drank that many cans in one night. I didn't even drink at all in those days!

We used to go to Mama's in Barkly Street, Footscray, near the Footscray Football Club and sit at the tables there or to Banana Alley in the city, near where the casino is now. It was called the Pieteria Café and they sold pies twenty-four hours a day. The boys respected us. No mucking around with other people's girlfriends or anything like that. Good people.

Later on, we kept in touch when Sharpie had a Cup Day barbecue or when we all caught up at the reunions. And weddings and of course, funerals—too many funerals.

In 1975, my mate, Ziggy, took me to a party at the Kensington flats where I met the members of the rock band AC/DC. They weren't famous then—they were really good and they hadn't hit the big time yet but they could party big time. We drank and had some fun with the girls at the party and I sat with Malcolm Young. We got along really well.

We both drank too much and got shit-faced together that night.

Malcolm Young of AC/DC circa 1975.

Malcolm was playing an old acoustic guitar and just messing around. There was a very well-endowed girl there in the flat and Malcolm teased me about her, then scratched a rude message about me and that girl into his guitar. He was just being drunk and silly and quite derogatory! He laughed and laughed at my expense. He thought it was a great joke, and then he gave me the guitar (which I still have).

We were to cross paths a number of times after that and we went to other parties of the same nature. I also went to the school in St Albans when they were playing there and went to say g'day but after that, they went on *Countdown* and fame caught hold of them—they were swept along to legend status after that. I wasn't really a fan though. I was just a drinking mate.

Poster advertising AC/DC's appearance at the local St Albans High School where David caught up with Malcolm again and hung out. AC/DC also appeared at Altona Hight School where kids came from far and wide to pack the hall and see them rock. Some locals complained that you could hear the band all over Altona.

Photos in a scrapbook kept by the Gibbons family.

Angels stop for gas before hitting the road circa 1968.

CHAPTER 11

ON THE ROAD

Riding a motorcycle is an independent thing. It's about the wind on your face and the freedom of the road. It's an independent thing that is great to do with your gang of friends.
— Anonymous

The Angels were never happier than when we were on a road trip. One time we went to Lakes Entrance and on the way there, one of the riders clipped a pedestrian who was walking on the side of the road in the dark. We all went back to see if he was okay and he said he was fine, but was obviously drunk, so we offered him a ride to make sure he didn't get hit again. He got on the back of one of our bikes and, as we took off, he came off the back and landed on his bum on the road. He decided he was much safer walking than trying to hang onto the back of a bike.

It was a great feeling to ride into a country town and see the locals' heads turn when they heard the sound of fifty

The Angels on a road trip. Roaring into a town and making heads turn was always a big buzz.

engines roaring. Some of the old blokes' faces filled with dread and some of the girls would smile and wave at us, happy to have a bit of excitement in the town.

The town's young blokes were not too happy with our presence and tried to throw their weight around sometimes. On one road trip, we camped near the river in Violet Town. Glenn and Chris went into town to have a drink at the pub and were at the bar when the guy next to him asked what they were doing in town. Glenn told him they were camping out by the river. The guy said, 'There is nothing better than camping out under the stars with a full moon and a big hard dick up ya arse!' Then it was on! Fists flew and others joined in the fray. There were some sore heads on both sides after that. The Angels never backed down from a fight when provoked.

Another road trip was from Williamstown to Adelaide to pick up an ex-police motorcycle I bought from an advertisement in the newspaper. I rode on the back of Sheepy's bike all the way there and it was a good ride. We had fun stopping at local cafés and towns to check out the local talent.

On the way back home, I rode my new Triumph 'Saint' motorcycle, but I hadn't prepared for the cold, wet, foggy weather that came rolling in. I was freezing, especially as I had a big hole in the crotch of my jeans and I was so cold that I sat on a heater in a café at Bordertown. I stuffed a newspaper down my pants and rode home with chilblains on my balls.

*

Blonde Margaret rode with the Angels and she remembers what life was like for a woman motorcycle rider in the early days:

> I grew up in Elwood and I used to hang around St Kilda near Luna Park and the Palais Theatre. The Angels and the Vikings were quite friendly and used to park their motorcycles on opposite sides of the road. It was there that I first saw a female rider riding in front of the Vikings. I could hear the noise of the engines and looked up to see a woman leading a group of motorcycle riders down the Esplanade. She looked just like Marlon Brando in *The Wild One* movie. I was so impressed, I remember thinking, 'How good is that!' and I began to save up to buy my own motorcycle.
>
> I got my learners permit at seventeen years and nine months old and bought a BSA Gold Flash 650 Twin which was quite a big bike and not what I had told my dad I was going to get. When I got home with my bike, he was not pleased. 'That doesn't look like a bloody Honda to me,' he complained.

I learnt to ride with a pillion passenger showing me to use the controls. The bike became an extension of my body and for a year I knocked around with some riders from Dandenong until, on one ride, I met the Angels on Beach Road.

The Angels were on their way to Arthurs Seat (a scenic 'lookout' in the hills) when my fellow rider and I met them, and they asked us to come too. That was when I met Meggsy, named after Ginger Meggs, the famous Australian cartoon character in the daily newspapers because his surname was Ginger.

Meggsy and I 'went together' for two or three years and I continued to ride with the Angels during that time. I bought a Triumph Tiger 10 and went to Bathurst in New South Wales for the motorcycle races every Easter with some of the boys.

When I first started knocking around with the Angels there was already another female riding with the Angels and later another girl, who was from the country, started riding with us.

On Saturday mornings, we would all ride through the Melbourne city streets and park our bikes on Elizabeth Street. There would be hundreds of bikes parked on the road outside the motorbike shops, the leather jacket shop and Vic Bogner's shop that did artwork on petrol tanks.

The boys would all go into the pub for a drink but this was a time when females were not allowed to drink in the public bar and we were excluded until one day, we marched into the public bar with the boys. The publican tried to throw us out but the Angels stood up for us, saying, 'Kick them out and we'll all go.' The publican backed down and we were allowed to stay from then on.

We were pretty much pioneers as far as girls riding motorbikes go in Melbourne in those days. You could count on one hand how many girls rode (in clubs/gangs) in the early 60s. We considered ourselves part of the Angels and we were treated as one of the boys. Although, in those days there were no equal rights and girls didn't usually get a membership disc, but we were proud Angels, nevertheless.

Some of the Angels used to knock around with Red Barons and ride to the motorbike rally at Ballarat. Ballarat is a big country town about an hour's ride from Melbourne. The boys used to go up there for the day and come home in the night. On one of these day trips, one of the Angels turned up on a shit heap of a bike that fell apart when it got there. When it came time to go home, the bike had no headlights or tail lights so the guys all rode at the front and the back of the one with no lights so he could get home safely. We looked out for each other.

Around this time, my good mate Tortoise had a claim to fame when he was asked to ride to a television station to watch *Countdown* being filmed. *Countdown* was the most popular music program in Australian TV history. It was broadcast nationwide on Australia's ABC, and was dedicated to Australian content, so it was responsible for helping a lot of Aussie singers and bands. It also featured overseas stars who were interviewed by Aussie music icon Molly Meldrum. Most young people in the 70s and 80s watched *Countdown*.

When Tortoise got the call from a mate to come to the studio on his motorbike, it was the night that famous international singer/star Meat Loaf was to appear on the show.

Meat Loaf had an edgy, tough bikie image and he planned to make a big entrance. He wanted to ride a motorcycle onto the stage but the producers were not happy with the safety aspects of that, so they got a few bikes and riders lined up for him to choose one to take him onto the stage.

Meat Loaf picked Tortoise out of the line-up and got on the back of his bike. Tortoise roared onto the set—shit-scared that Meat Loaf would fall off the back of the bike and hurt himself.

Tortoise said, 'My afro hair was so big that it went on stage five minutes before Meat Loaf did!'

Tortoise and Meat Loaf on the Countdown *set, 1978.*

top: A host of Angels on the move.
bottom: Boys and their bikes, circa 1969.

CHAPTER 12

ROAD RASH

Faster, faster, faster, until the thrill of speed overcomes the fear of death.
— Hunter S. Thompson

I used to ride with mates who were not Angels, too. When I was about seventeen, I was riding my motorbike at Altona with a group of other boys when we saw a group of girls on the pier. We wanted to make a big impression, so we rode our bikes along the pier to make a grand entrance.

We picked up a couple of them and they got on the back of our bikes. We headed down the pier into the waiting arms of the local constabulary. We got booked for riding on the pier and they told us to piss off.

After that we went to the sewerage farm at Werribee to hang out. Peter Shultz was skidding around, just being a dickhead, when his front mudguard fell over the front wheel and he lost control.

He fell off his bike and got covered in gravel rash. One of the girls put tissues over his bleeding skin and the tissues stuck to the wounds. He went home to soak in the bath to get them off, but the gravel was embedded in his skin and he had to go to the hospital. There they put him in an antiseptic bath and scrubbed him with a scrubbing brush to get the stones out.

I could hear him yelling from the next room.

His jacket was, literally, a bloody mess and his mum went out and got him a new one straight away. I got his old jacket and took it home. I washed it, let it dry, put 'dubbing' on it, and it was good as new. I wore that jacket for many years.

Motorcycle injuries were, and still are, common. A nineteen-year-old apprentice boilermaker had his right leg amputated after a collision with a car in Geelong Road. He was riding as a pillion passenger when the accident happened, leaving him with multiple fractures to his arms and facial injuries as well.

Accidents were, and still are, common. Peter Honda recalled an accident that was very unusual:

> Normie AJ had damaged a leg in a motorcycle accident and had to have it amputated but he could still ride okay. One day we were all riding together for a funeral and we turned around a corner. As we did, his fake leg fell off. Normie AJ had lost his same leg twice. We had a good laugh at that and he could see the funny side too.

I've had my share of accidents. When I was about sixteen, my mate Richard bought a 1962 FE Holden from a dealer in Footscray. He had the car a couple of months when we went cruising, looking for girls around the local area. We ended up at Fleet Wing's in Laverton for a burger and Coke and then made our way home along Queen Street. Richard wanted to try out the speed of the car and, as there were no houses in the area, he planted his foot and got the car up to about ninety miles per hour. We went around a slight curve in the road at Merton Street and the steering arm broke off the steering box, making Richard lose control of the car. We crashed through a power pole, down a culvert and through a small bluestone wall. The car ended up in a paddock on the side of the road, broken into two pieces with only the roof holding it together.

Fleet Wing's Cafe, Laverton.

We had some horrendous injuries. The engine was in the passenger-side front seat breaking both of Peter Shultz's legs and some of his ribs and it also took the top of his head and some of his face off. I was in the back seat on the passenger side and we were both trapped in the car. The car was burning as a cattle truck pulled up and the driver got out and put out the fire with dirt before helping Richard and my brother Glenn out of the car. They were shaken and Glenn had a broken collarbone, and Richard had facial injuries, but they were not seriously injured.

The driver of the cattle truck then turned his attention to Peter and to me. He tried to pull us free but we were trapped. He called an ambulance on his CB radio and the police arrived. When they saw the car, the police thought they were attending a fatality but, thanks to the quick reaction of that Good Samaritan, Peter and I got cut out of the wreck and to hospital in time to save our lives.

I never saw that cattle truck driver again and never even knew his name, but I will always remember him and be grateful to him.

I was in an induced coma for two weeks and in hospital for about three and a half months with a fractured skull and both my legs in traction. To pass the time I used to roll bandages but when the Red Cross woman came to visit, she asked if I would like to do something more interesting and try sewing moccasins. I was glad of something to keep me busy and over the next few months made lots of moccasins. She would bring the cut-out shapes and I would sew them together. Peter 'put shit on me' for doing that but he soon started making them too.

Peter and I shared a ward with two other guys and one night, one of them climbed out the window and went to the pub to buy beer. We gave him money to get us some as well. The next morning, the matron read the riot act when she saw the empty beer cans on the floor, and said, 'I have never seen such a disgusting spectacle!' I think we took that as a challenge!

As soon as we were feeling better, we started harassing the nurses. They were young and we were young, cheeky and horny. One nurse paid us back for being cheeky and painted the soles of our feet with Mercurochrome for a joke! Everyone who came into the room would ask why we had red feet. We never confessed though.

Those poor nurses were happy to see the back of us, except for one. Peter was keen on one of the young nurses and he would try to kiss her at every opportunity. She would push him away and laugh but you could tell she liked him. One night she snuck into the ward. Peter was flat on his back and in traction as she climbed on top of him and made all his dreams come true. All I could do was watch in envy.

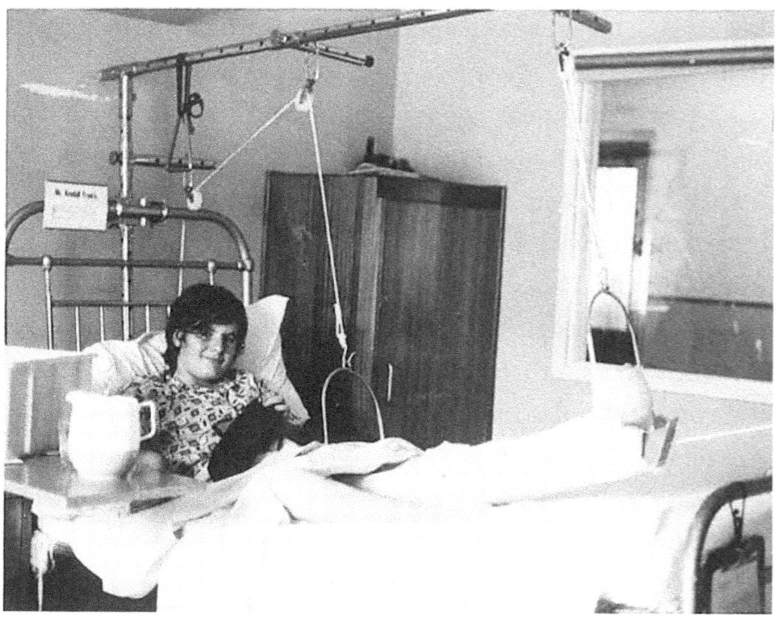

The accident didn't stop us taking risks and testing ourselves out on the roads. Street races were common back then. We raced motorcycles in New Street, Newport, and practised doing wheel stands. When the Westgate Bridge was being built, before it was joined in the middle, we used to race up and down the bridge.

The police tried to catch us a few times and eventually they did. They pulled the fuel lines off our motorbikes and told us to piss off, which we did … but not for long. We went back many times. It was our track—a place where we could practise our skills.

A few of us went to the Royal Melbourne Showgrounds and saw Evel Knievel. He was an American stunt rider who rode motorcycles and did amazing jumps. Of course, we headed straight to Hall Street in Spotswood to practise wheel stands and standing on the seat and letting go of the handlebars. It was a bit of a competition to see who could do the tricks the best. The local residents must have got sick of the racket because the police inevitably arrived and we just pissed off.

As well as street racing, David competed at Santapod in England and at Calder in Victoria on his Triumph.

In 1978, I had a Triumph that I built up into a drag bike. Later I put a Weslake motor in it and raced mainly at Calder. I had a lot of fun and a bit of success until they brought in Japanese bikes that I couldn't compete against.

I didn't have much of a career because I lost control at Calder and ran into the wall. I broke my right leg in that smash and the front bone was sticking out the front of my shin. It hurt like hell. I sold the bike to a fella from Geelong who was later killed on it, so I guess I was lucky.

Peter Schultz and my mate, Ivan, both raced their bikes on the street. Ivan had a twin-engine Kawasaki that he raced at Calder too and Peter was always there to help out with the bike at home or in the pits.

There were a few places that we frequented at different times for street racing. An undeveloped area often used for street races was Industrial Avenue in Werribee. Local kids gathered there, drank, took drugs and raced their cars and bikes up and down the street for fun.

In 1975, my brother Glenn was hanging out with my brother Dale and some other guys. Glenn was tripping and decided to get on someone else's bike to race without his helmet. He lost control and smashed his head onto the edge of the footpath and the bike skidded into the crowd, breaking bystander's legs and causing other injuries.

There was only one ambulance with one driver/ambulanceman at Werribee Hospital, so he was running around trying to attend to the crowd while Glenn lay on the ground unconscious. Glenn stayed unconscious and on life support for a week before it was decided he would not survive. They had to pull the plug and it broke our hearts.

He is buried in Williamstown Cemetery with our baby brother, Paul, who had died at six weeks of age. Their tombstone features a motorcyclist with a child passenger on the back.

Glenn King (1956–1975).

BIKES CAN BE FUN OR…[1]

A bare-headed motorcycle rider was very seriously injured and two on-lookers badly hurt last Wednesday night when Glenn King, of Werribee, was thrown from his motorcycle.

Glenn King's brother, Dale, who saw the accident but escaped injury, dropped in at The Banner the other day in the hope that a report on Glenn's accident might shake other riders out of their complacency, and possibly prevent further occurrences of this type of accident.

---

1 The Werribee Banner, 1975.

They turned off his life support a few days after that article was published. That day I lost my little brother. He was my best friend. My constant companion. A piece of me.

Rest in Peace—Glenn.

My mum was such a gentle woman and I never saw her get angry at anyone until the day of Glenn's funeral. It happened when the cavalcade of motorbikes left the church on their way to the cemetery and travelled past a parked police car on the side of the road. The policemen laughed, pointed, cheered and waved as my brother's coffin passed.

Mum's grief just exploded. She had lost her nineteen-year-old son and the police disrespected her grief. They didn't even know who was in that coffin. The cops were just reacting to the cavalcade of motorbikes and jeering and cheering that a bikie was dead.

Later she made a formal complaint to the Chief Commissioner of Police and those coppers got into deep shit for their disgusting behaviour. Mum got an official, written apology from the Chief Commissioner, though she could never forgive them.

Angel—Tommy Garner (right), pictured with friends.

Motorcycle accidents happen often. People in cars don't see motorcyclists, and motorcyclists of varying degrees of expertise can often find themselves in trouble on the road. There were lots of accidents where riders ended up in hospital. Two of the Angels were involved in an accident on Geelong Road when a car collided with them. The bike rider had multiple fractures and facial injuries while the pillion passenger lost his leg. Some Angels died in accidents and are still mourned by the group.

One such member was Tommy Garner who lost his life on the road in 1962.

Tommy worked as a jockey on a furniture truck making deliveries for Maples of Footscray. The local kids were in awe of his Elvis-style hair and leather jacket. This is his eulogy as it appeared in the local paper:

GUARD OF "ANGELS"[2]

Riding High

Tommy migrated here with his mother, father and young brother Robert three years ago.

He worked as a truck driver for a Footscray manufacturer, but at night and at most weekends, he was out on his motorbike riding with his new friends.

Most of the Angels who come from the Footscray-Williamstown district are young fellows aged from 17 to 22. They wear on their jackets the brass disc with the word "Angel" engraved in red across it.

When a friend was killed in the motorcycle smash recently, Tommy told his father and his pals if he were killed in a similar smash, he would like to have a motorcycle escort at his funeral.

---

2 Original clipping provided by Mrs Gibbons.

"I would like motorbikes to come with me on my last ride," he told them.

Mr Henry Garner was pleased today when about 40 Angels arrived outside the funeral parlour in Droop Street, Footscray. Most of the boys were wearing their best suits.

A member of the Angels said it had been agreed to collect £100 in the next month to pay for a headstone for Tommy's grave.

And today they sent along a big white and orange wreath made in the shape of a motorcycle.

As this wreath was placed on top of his coffin 25 motorcycle engines thundered to life and took up formation.

The Angels were carrying out a comrade's wish to accompany him on his last ride.

My good mate from childhood, Peter Schultz, wasn't an Angel in any sense of the word and he didn't have a mentor like Johnny Wilde to look out for him. Eventually, he got deeply involved in drugs and started dealing. In 1988, he was murdered.

His body was found in a car beside the Maribyrnong River in Footscray. He had been given a lethal dose of heroin and the scene was staged to look like a suicide with a hose from the exhaust pipe into the window.

In truth, he owed the wrong people drug money.

RIP Peter Schultz.

David's jacket with patches—Angels Motorcycle Club, Buell motorcycles and his military service patch.

CHAPTER 13

THE END OF AN ERA

We stand alone together.
— *Band of Brothers*, HBO TV Miniseries, 2001

The Hells Angels motorcycle gang was originally formed in California in 1948 when a group of World War II veterans started riding together as they struggled to cope with their return to civilian life. They quickly gained popularity throughout America, then internationally, and soon became the biggest motorcycle gang in the world.

There is no international or national boss. Each 'chapter' has a president, a vice-president, a sergeant-at-arms, a road captain, secretary/treasurer, and security officer. Full members wear 'colours' of two rocker patches on their backs: a curved 'Hells Angels' patch across the top and a second across the bottom identifies their chapter or territory.

Hells Angels' first international chapter was in Auckland, New Zealand in 1961 and the first Australian chapters were admitted in the 70s.

For a time, the new chapter of Hells Angels and the local Angels co-existed but it was inevitable that a takeover would be broached. The Angels' philosophy was very different to that of Hells Angels. The local Angels had no business interests and were not about anything other than having a good time.

Eventually the members had to choose—amalgamate or leave.

Some members chose to retire while others joined up and became part of the Hells Angels.

The Angels' band of brothers still kept in touch. How could we share so many good and bad times and let that go? The following article by Mary-Ellen Ryan appeared in the local press in 1989:

WILD NO LONGER

Angels wing in more than 300 bikers, men and women, who once struck fear into the hearts of model citizens gathered in Rockbank Hall on Melbourne Cup Day. With them were their spouses, children and, in many cases, grandchildren. They were there to celebrate the 25th anniversary of the Western Suburbs Angels Motorcycle Club. With an average age between 45 and 50, the Angels of yesteryear started celebrating about 8am Tuesday morning—and continued until sometimes Wednesday afternoon.

The reunion was the culmination of 12 month's work by organiser John Wilde, father of nine, grandfather of two who now lives in retirement in Melton. "You see some major changes, especially when you haven't seen some of these people for 25 years," Mr Wilde said. "There was major hair loss, major hair colour change and major stomachs."

The Angels began sometime in the 50s, with the bulk of the membership from Footscray and Altona. Members modelled themselves on the Marlon Brando–style of biker portrayed in the movie classic, "The Wild One" disdainful of the later Easy Rider clones.

The Angels suffered at the hands of the media according to Mr Wilde, who said much of the adverse publicity was "unwarranted".

"We had a mutual interest in motorcycles," he said. "In the days when pubs closed at 6 o'clock, the Angels would congregate outside a milk bar in Barkly Street near Footscray Football Club, or on the beach front at Williamstown. Mr Wilde said, "Every night and every weekend, between 30 and 40 club members would gather, riding mostly English bikes like Triumph, BSA or AJS. They are collectors' items now," he said.

Two Angels arrived at the reunion on motorcycles, but Mr Wilde noted they were updated versions of the machines that the group used to ride. "They were hard on the piles," he said.

Mr Wilde said he had managed to contact all but 10 per cent of the original membership. They came from Perth and Darwin, and one even flew in from the Philippines for the reunion. Another Angel, who has come a long way from the days outside the Barkly Street milk bar, piloted his own plane from the Gold Coast. The Gold Coast and South East Queensland proved to be an attraction for many of the group's members, who came back from there to Rockbank Hall.

According to Mr Wilde, the Angels were fond of impromptu weekend trips to Sydney or Deniliquin. Not much was done in the way of planning and distance was obviously no object. One of their favourite rallying points he said, was Truganina, between Werribee and Laverton. "We would get right out of everybody's way," he said. "We

> **would pull up and light a bonfire and have a big party." Mr Wilde thinks the Angels' parties were then a lot milder than anything that goes on today.**
>
> **He said, "Bikers received a lot of publicity in those days, primarily because of the big biker funerals which attracted a lot of people on big bikes. We lost quite a few members," he said. The men and women who survived those days on their large bikes are now scheduled to celebrate in the same fashion until 1994. Rockbank Hall has been prebooked for Melbourne Cup Day for the next five years, and Mr Wilde is already planning a major celebration for the 30th anniversary.**

The Angels were no longer a club, but they gathered together for reunions to relive the heady days of Sunbury Rock Festival and organised a festival of our own in '96, '97, '98 and '99.

Johnny Wilde had a farm at Mount Doran, which provided the perfect venue for a reunion. We got a permit from the fire brigade and organised for food to be available all day and most of the night. Food vans serving baked potatoes, bacon and eggs, sandwiches, hotdogs, hamburgers, and a twenty-foot refrigeration container kept the food chilled and fresh. By this time, we were no longer teenagers but family men, so we invited kids, wives and partners, and planned fun for young and old. In keeping with our philosophy, we didn't want to make money for ourselves. Instead we looked for a charity to support with the profits from the weekends and decided to support the Starlight Foundation to help kids with cancer.

The Mount Doran reunions were held over long weekends in the late 90s. Old members of the Angels and their friends and families camped in tents or caravans or slept in cars. There were fires to sit around and talk motorcycles and cars or relive our glory days. It was a good time to catch up on who was doing what. Continuing the Angels' attitude of 'inclusiveness', tickets were sold to anyone who wanted to come along and raise money for charity and have a good time.

It was a family event and the kids and partners were all welcomed and entertained with fun activities. A favourite was the greasy pig race. A squealing piglet would be covered in Vaseline and released so the kids could try to catch it. The kids scrambled and squealed as much as the pig and as soon as one kid got hold of the little porker, it squirmed out of the grasp and was off again with the kids chasing it until they either got tired, got the pig or it got away.

We also played a game called Cow Lotto. One of the paddocks was marked off into a grid with numbers and the boys purchased a section each. A cow wandered in the field and when it crapped on a section of the grid, that person got the prize money.

The guys came up with an idea to find out how long it would take for a car engine to blow up without oil. We took bets on how long it would take and then put a brick on the gas pedal of an old car and let it go full pelt until it went 'boom'!

Later, when the kids were in bed, the adult entertainment began. There were strippers 'with benefits' for both the men and women who wanted to engage in that kind of activity. For others, the live music, plenty of booze and good company was enough to while away the evenings.

top: Johnny's property at Mount Doran. One of many reunion weekends organised to get the Angels and their families together and to raise money for charity. All proceeds went to help sick kids.

bottom: Photograph of a commemorative wine bottle from an Angels' reunion, courtesy of Dean Gilbert.

Reunions were held once a year at different locations and venues. There were dinner dances and barbecues and other get-togethers which were usually family-oriented and always fun. The dinner dances were not the 'old-time' type of dinner dance that our parents approved of. They were more rock'n'roll! Great music and dancing, and although most of the blokes didn't go in for that kind of thing, the ladies enjoyed it.

Members of the Vigilantes (from the Pascoe Vale area) and Derelicts (from the western suburbs) came along to our events as well. There were 'cross-over' events where they were welcome, just like we were welcome at some of their events too. We supported their dinner dances and attended their other events because we had lots of mates in those clubs and we all still liked to party where there was live music.

top: Motorcycles parked near the stage at Mount Doran ready for the bands to begin playing.

bottom: Johnny's property at Mount Doran. The Angels raising money for charity and renewing friendships—reliving the heady days of their youth.

David's jacket with Mount Doran reunion patches.

Ex-Angels gather to celebrate a wedding. The wedding of an ex-Angel, 'Powelly', circa 1990 where a lot of the boys renewed friendships and relived old times.

David from the age of eighteen and a few of his rides.

CHAPTER 14

DIFFERENT ROADS

As I approve of a youth that has something of the old man in him, so I am no less pleased with an old man that has something of the youth. He that follows this rule may be old in body, but can never be so in mind.
— Marcus Tullius Cicero

After the Angels went their different ways, I joined the Australian Army—Royal Australian Regiment. I was in the infantry, surrounded by a different band of brothers.

I enjoyed the regimentation and discipline that the army offered. The training was harsh—they broke us down to mould us into the way of the military, but I coped okay with the shouting and humiliation they dealt out to recruits, and I enjoyed the company of our unit. I also enjoyed learning new skills and drinking gallons of cheap alcohol. The army made lots of alcoholics as there was not much else to do when we were off-duty—just drink or smoke.

By this time, I was married to Leanne and had a child and, although I missed my little family, I knew they were safe at the in-law's place. Once, while on leave at home for a few days, I said to Leanne, 'I don't mind the soldier's life but it's so bloody cold on sentry duty.'

Leanne opened her underwear drawer and produced a pair of green knitted tights, saying, 'Try wearing these under your uniform.'

Back at the barracks I started to put on the tights. 'What the fuck are you wearing them for?' said one of the guys.

'It's freezing on sentry duty and I'm going to do something about it!'

Soon all the boys were coming in to take a look and have a laugh. I just told them to piss off and went on duty. Within a week they were all wearing tights under their uniforms!

I became very fit and enjoyed the physical and mental challenges the army set for us. The army had held a fascination with me for a long time and I worked hard at becoming a good soldier.

I had previously tried to join the army when I was just sixteen years old. Peter Schultz and I thought it would be good to join up and go to fight for our country in Vietnam, so we 'borrowed' my friend's birth certificate and Peter's older brother's birth certificate, and went to enlist. The officer took one look at me and knew I was underage. He sent us packing with 'Get out of here before I kick your arse!' and I had to wait until I was twenty-one to join up.

My uncle Ron had fought in World War II and I respected and admired him. He was a kind and gentle man and when people tried to blame my old man's viciousness on 'the war', I always reconciled in my mind that it was nothing to do with that. Uncle Ron had suffered through the war, serving in Tobruk,

New Guinea, and the islands north of Australia, and came home gentle, if not unscathed.

After the army, I stayed in the Army Reserves and went to work at the naval dockyards in Williamstown with another of my mother's brothers, Uncle Jack. My Uncle Jack was one of the bosses in the dockyard and he got me a job as a casual to begin with. The other blokes were a bit cautious at first and scared to say anything in front of me in case I was a nark, but it didn't take them long to work out I was almost as bad as they were.

The first day they gave me an easy job to do. They told me to drive a truck to collect some gas cylinders and take them to the bottle compound. I came back two hours later and was 'told off' in no uncertain terms because the job was supposed to last until the next day. If I worked quickly I would 'make the other drivers look bad', so I had to hide for the rest of the day. I hid in the bottle shed and had a snooze until knock-off time.

The dockyard was another place where I felt like I was hanging out with my mates every day. There were lots of interesting characters at the dockyards—and there was quite a mixture of morals represented there.

There was a funny, little bloke on the docks who was an ex-boxer. He was about five-feet tall, had cauliflower ears and his nose was all over his face. He had a nervous twitch that made him wrinkle his nose and turn his head to one side constantly. He made us all laugh when he came around with watches strapped up both of his arms and in his pockets. He seemed to have an endless supply of watches. He would say, 'If you don't want a watch, do you want some nice jewellery for the missus … get in sweet with her?'

On the docks, it was common to use company time for personal work. 'Rabbits' was what we called personal jobs we did during work time. People used to bring in bundles of steel and timber to make all sorts of things for themselves. The people on the gate never worried if a bloke brought in some rough old timber and walked out with a lovely table or a rocking horse. They might bring in some old metal scraps and take out a boat anchor made from pristine materials!

There was a magnificent yacht built at the docks—lovely wood and beautiful design. When it was finished, someone just sailed it away, never to be seen again.

One of the bosses got a shipment of steel to make a sixty-foot by forty-foot garage on his property. Not only did he get it delivered by truck from the docks, but he got six of the blokes to go to his house and erect the garage!

Two major thefts involved the disappearance of a truck load of silver solder. That just went missing. The other huge theft was of a brand-new bobcat on a truck—both of which disappeared into thin air.

It was common practice, too, to go to the pub at lunch time and sometimes stay for the whole afternoon. Your mates would clock you off at the end of the shift. The Pier Hotel, the Oriental, Prince of Wales and The Britannia all benefited from the dockyard workers' lunch-time custom and at knock-off time the pubs would be full as a boot as well.

The worst incident on the docks happened when I was in the crowd at the gates for a union meeting. I was listening to speeches from union representatives when a car drove by spraying bullets into the crowd. I ducked for cover but a couple of blokes got injured. There was front page news the next day about the violence from different factions on the docks.

The Painters and Dockers were infamous with good reason. There were some really 'hard' men on the docks but some really good blokes too and lifelong friendships began there and continued through good times and bad.

I drove trucks locally and interstate for the dockyard and eventually was given the task of driving the Naval Commodore who was in charge of the dockyards. My mates put shit on me because I had to wear a suit every day: 'Look at Mr Fancy Pants!'

After working for the Commodore, I drove for Bill Millen, who became General Manager of the dockyard. He told me to call him Bill when we were alone but Mr Mill when we were on official duties. He had come from Canada to Australia to manage the dockyard and you couldn't find a nicer man. He treated me extremely well and even invited my wife and I to attend cocktail parties and a Christmas party at his house with other admirals and dignitaries.

After the dockyard was privatised and I was retrenched, I went to work for Ansett driving interstate coaches. It was a pretty solitary kind of life even though I was surrounded by passengers; there was no camaraderie except occasionally at the bus stops where I might catch up with another driver.

Patch on the overalls worn by dock workers. In fact, a lot of people in Williamstown owned a pair of these overalls that had 'fallen off the back of a truck'.

It was common for long distance drivers to swallow pills to keep them awake—the company supplied them. It was hard being away from home all the time, travelling for long hours and away for days, then coming home to try to sleep with (by this time) two babies in the house and uppers in my system. It was even harder on my wife. It was a lonely life for her, even though she had her family for support.

*

It was during this time in 1990 that I found out I had cancer. In fact, all the men I had worked with at the dockyard to transport toxic waste from naval ships to a rubbish tip in Newport got sick too. We all battled our various cancers while trying to battle the Australian Government for compensation, but that was not forthcoming. Legal loopholes and our 'lost' medical records that were scurried away by men in black suits meant none of us got compensation. All records were 'disappeared'.

After a time of ill health, I went to work for the State Government driving various trucks and machinery until I was asked to drive for the Governor of Victoria and be part of his security. I felt honoured to be asked to fill such a role and I was able to put to good use all the skills I had learned during my time in the army. That new role meant I was a driver for many visiting dignitaries, including politicians and royalty.

Working for the Governor of Victoria, Davis McCaughey, was a great job that I loved. I looked after his car and drove him and his wife to lots of official and private functions. We got to know each other really well and I had great respect for him.

Dr McCaughey was a good and kind man of principle and I enjoyed looking after him. He would bring his lunch from the dining room in Government House to sit at the kitchen table with me while I was eating lunch and discuss anything and everything. I like to think we became more than driver and Governor. I like to think we became friends.

While working for the Governor I was required to drive royalty and other dignitaries who visited or stayed at Government House. One of those visiting dignitaries, the leader of a foreign country, gave me the task of driving two of his wives into the city to go shopping. I took them to Myer and David Jones and it was like trying to corral cats! They ran everywhere, looking at the clothes and buying everything they could find! What a few days I had trying to keep track of them and carrying all their shopping bags back to the car. That visiting dignitary gave me a gold watch for taking care of him and his wives while he was in Australia. In fact, he gave presents to all the staff who made his stay pleasant.

Melbourne Cup Racing Carnival was always a very busy time for me. Members of the Royal family and other visitors from overseas stayed at Government House and I was required to ferry them back and forth from Government House to the race track. Needless to say, much champagne was consumed and guards were let down in the back seats on the return journey in the car. It's surprising how many people forget there is a driver in the car who can see and hear them.

When US President George Bush Senior came to Melbourne, I was required to work alongside his staff and the US Secret Service.

On the way to the old casino in Flinders Street, protesting students threw a brick at his car which luckily missed its target. After the official gathering at the casino, we drove to Melbourne University where President Bush was presented with an award.

While our passengers were inside, the cars were parked and we went to get some lunch. We were away from the cars for ten minutes and came back to discover that the students had rubbed human excrement all over the cars. The police who were with us said we were not to retaliate in any way, but the American security guys had other ideas. They caught some of the protesters running from the scene with poo on their hands and smacked them about, rubbing one bloke's face into the poo on the cars. The girl with him got off more lightly—they let her run off without giving chase.

We were left to try to clean the cars with handtowels as best we could. It was pretty disgusting.

Governor McCaughey and his wife were just lovely people and I was devastated when my cancer came back and I had to stop working for them.

After treatment in 1997, I went back to work for the new Governor, James Gobbo. He was our first Governor of Italian descent and also the first Catholic to be sworn in as Governor. He too was a good man.

While I worked for Government House, I had to do an anti-terrorism driving course to make sure I could protect the Governor and his family in an emergency. This I really enjoyed as it was almost as exciting as riding my Harley.

Luckily, I didn't have to use my anti-terrorism driving skills. My job was mostly to take Mrs Gobbo to fulfil her duties at her many official engagements. That was short-lived as my health failed again.

After that, there were doctors and chemo and lots of hospital stays but there were other jobs at times when I was well enough. Almost all of them involved working with engines or driving.

I was working as a diesel mechanic for a tractor company when I was carrying a battery and slipped on some oil. As I my feet came out from under me, I put one hand back to stop my fall, still holding the battery in the other hand. Unfortunately, I couldn't save myself and my wrist was crushed. I had to give up riding my Harley after that because a steel plate in my wrist meant I could no longer bend it or confidently control the handbrake. After years of riding motorbikes, I turned to my second love—fast cars.

In recent times I have been rebuilding a drag car and a hot rod with the help of some old mates from the dockyards. Unfortunately, there are no materials confiscated from the docks these days!

Other people from the dockyards and the members of the Angels went on to work in a variety of roles and we have remained friends through the years, regularly catching up on each other's news and reliving the folly of youth.

The dockyard has a reunion every year while the Angels' members no longer have formal get-togethers.

A lot of the Angels have gone now but the ones who are still around keep in touch with Johnny.

We like to hang out and talk about the old days and rekindle our enduring love of motorcycles and vintage cars. Johnny always has a new project or an old one to revisit in the garage. While we were being interviewed for the local newspaper in 2020, Johnny said:

> David and I still get together and look at our cars or bikes. I've owned hundreds of bikes over the years.

> I used to get the paper and go around to the houses and put a five-dollar deposit on all of them so they wouldn't sell to anyone else and then decide which ones to go and get. I did them up and sold them. Lots of them.
>
> I still love bikes and I love cars too. I've had lots of fantastic cars. I still have my 1965 Thunderbird—I got that at a Formosa swap meet in the States. I have two limousines for my business and I still have a Harley. My children say I'm still a hoon!
>
> The best thing about the Angels was that we were all mates and we are still all mates. They ring me out of the blue from Adelaide or Sale or wherever they are now and we catch up for a few days. The same guys I hung around with when I was twenty-five are still my friends at seventy-five.

We are all old blokes now and have other lives and priorities, but we still phone each other or stop for a coffee or a yarn when we bump into each other on the street. When that happens, the memories come flooding back and we are Angels again.

David's jacket may have been hung up, but he remains an Angel.

BIBLIOGRAPHY

Australian Harley Riders. Accessed 14 August 2020. hdoz.org.au

Dower, Alan. 'Juvenile Violence'. *Melbourne Truth*, 24 February 1962.

Dower, Alan. '"The Wild Ones" On Beaches.' *The Truth*, 13 January 1962.

Gibbons, Margarite. Angels newspaper scrapbook holder.

Kelly, Ned. Ned Kelly to Joe Byrne, 1879. 'The Jerilderie Letter'.

Kuipers, Richard. 'Petersen (1974)'. Accessed 29 July 2020. https://aso.gov.au/titles/features/petersen/notes/

'Police Halt "Angels" Street Party.' *The Sun*, 9 April 1962.

'Police to Break Up Packs.' *The Sun*, 22 February 1962.

ACKNOWLEDGEMENTS

Johnny Wilde, Bob McKean, Margarite Gibbons, Cheryl Urch, Rachel Pavey, Kim Walsh, Glen Hyde, Ken McLeod, Michelle Micallef, John Scott, Rodney Neyland, Kriss Oliver, Mark Phillips, Deborah Gough, Margaret Buchanan, Stuart Hart.

Cover design: Patrick Walsh.

Johnny and David catching up in 2020.

ABOUT THE AUTHORS

David King was only ten years old when he met the Angels and that chance meeting would change David's life. David found, in the Angels, a group of older boys and men who shared his love of motorcycles and his need to belong.

David grew up, married Williamstown nurse, Leanne O'Brien, and they raised three children, sharing their lives until Leanne was tragically lost to cancer. David met Maureen Lane in 2012. They married in 2015 and continued their life journey together. They live in the Victorian seaside suburb of Altona, close to the old racecourse and the paddocks where the Angels used to gather. Maureen spends her time writing stories while David continues to make engines roar.

Maureen Lane grew up in Yarraville where she enjoyed an ideal childhood as the product of a loving home. When she met David King, Maureen was fascinated by his story and the contrast to her own childhood. She believed David's story is an important snapshot of life in the 50s, 60s and 70s when social norms were in flux and rebels stood up for the freedom to live as they chose.

Maureen set about writing David's story with him in order to acknowledge the Angels and to cement the Angels' place in history. Maureen loves to listen to people's stories and has a passion for recording the history that others have forgotten. Her previous published books include: *Pubs, Punts & Pastures, a History of Pioneer Irish Women on the Saltwater River* (with Joan Carstairs), *A Patchwork of Memories* (Altona & Surrounds) and *Putting the Fun Back into Drag Racing.*

top: David centre stage at Mount Doran in signature white t-shirt.
bottom: Maureen with David on a Harley June, 2020. Courtesy of Goya Dmytryshchak.

www.ingramcontent.com/pod-product-compliance
Ingram Content Group UK Ltd.
Pitfield, Milton Keynes, MK11 3LW, UK
UKHW020227250726
13967UKWH00001B/223